DURON BELL

DuRon's Guide to Living the Dream

Helping my People Escape the Matrix in Style, Since 2018

This book was professionally typeset on Reedsy.
Find out more at reedsy.com

Contents

Introduction

My fellow citizens of planet Earth, today I want to talk to you about a concept that's becoming increasingly significant among those who dare to dream big and think outside the box—"escaping the matrix." Now, what do we mean by this? The "matrix" refers to the traditional American dream, that familiar path many of us have been told to follow. It's a path where you work diligently, often sacrificing your passions and personal time, until you reach your mid-60s. And after decades of hard work, you retire, hoping to enjoy your golden years. But all too often, these years are spent in environments that can feel unfriendly and burdensome, where your hard-earned savings don't go as far as they should, and where the quality of life isn't what you envisioned.

Let's be real here, folks. We've been sold this idea that you grind your whole life, get a gold watch at retirement, and then spend your twilight years wondering why you didn't enjoy the ride a bit more. It's like working 40 years to buy a ticket to a movie that's already half over. That's not living—that's surviving.

Escaping the matrix is about breaking free from this conventional mold. It's about challenging the status quo and reimagining what your life can be. It's about taking the resources you've accumulated over years of hard work—your savings, investments, and other assets—and using them in ways that allow you to live more fully, more richly, and more wisely. This means leveraging your financial resources in environments where you can maximize their value, where you can short the dollar or benefit from an advantageous exchange rate. The goal is to live a life that surpasses the North American standard at a fraction of the cost.

Now, I can hear some of you saying, "DuRon, this sounds too good to be true!" But let me break it down for you. Imagine retiring not to a life of limitations and financial anxiety, but to a world where your dollars stretch further, where you can enjoy a higher standard of living, and where the environment is welcoming and enriching. It's about smart, strategic choices that let you live with dignity, freedom, and a renewed sense of purpose.

Picture this: You move to a place where your retirement savings can afford you luxuries that would be out of reach back home. You're sipping margaritas on a beach while your friends back home are shoveling snow. That's what I'm talking about! It's about taking control of your destiny, making informed decisions, and setting yourself up for a future where you can truly thrive.

Consider for a moment the possibilities. You could find yourself living in a vibrant, culturally rich community where the cost of living is a fraction of what it is in the United States. Your retirement savings could afford you luxuries and comforts that would be out of reach back home. You'd have access to high-quality healthcare, beautiful surroundings, and a lifestyle that emphasizes well-being and personal fulfillment. It's about taking control of your destiny, making informed decisions, and setting yourself up for a future where you can truly thrive.

Imagine telling your friends, "Yeah, I moved to the Dominican Republic. My dollar goes further, the sun's always shining, and the only thing I'm shoveling is sand off my porch." That's a whole new level of flex, my friends.

Now, let's not forget the broader implications of this shift. By embracing the global community, you're not just improving your own life—you're contributing to a more interconnected, understanding world. You're building bridges, fostering relationships, and promoting a spirit of global citizenship that is so crucial in today's world. You're showing that we can live harmoniously, learn from each other, and create communities that celebrate diversity and inclusion.

So let's break those chains, challenge the status quo, and step into a brighter, more promising future. It's time to think big, act boldly, and embrace the vast possibilities that lie beyond our traditional borders. We can truly become global!

WHAT IS ESCAPING THE MATRIX?

My fellow Americans, imagine a different kind of life—one that breaks free from the confines of the traditional American dream. The term "escaping the matrix" represents this very idea: stepping out of the conventional path laid out for us and embracing a new way of living, one that prioritizes freedom, adventure, and financial security.

In the United States, many of us are familiar with the narrative that tells us to work hard until our mid-60s, then retire and hopefully enjoy the fruits of our labor. But this story often falls short of its promise. Social Security, once a reliable safety net, is now facing significant challenges. Reports from the Social Security Administration indicate that funds could be depleted by the 2030s if no action is taken. This uncertainty leaves many of us wondering whether the system we've been contributing to for decades will be there when we need it most.

Now, consider the story of Jack and Jane, a couple from Michigan. After working tirelessly for over 40 years, they found themselves facing retirement with concerns about their financial future. Social Security benefits were modest, and the cost of living in the U.S. was high. They felt trapped in a system that no longer seemed to serve their needs. Determined to find a better way, they began researching alternatives and discovered the concept of living abroad as expats.

Jack and Jane decided to move to Mexico, a country with a lower cost of living and a vibrant expat community. By leveraging their savings and Social Security benefits, they were able to afford a lifestyle that was not only comfortable but luxurious compared to their previous standard of living in the U.S. They found a beautiful home, had access to excellent healthcare, and enjoyed a rich cultural experience—all for a fraction of what they would have paid back home.

This is the essence of escaping the matrix. It's about taking your hard-earned resources and using them in an environment where you can stretch your dollar further. By doing so, you can achieve a quality of life that might seem out of reach if you remain confined to the traditional path. Imagine investing in countries where the cost of living is significantly lower, where you can benefit from favorable exchange rates, and where your money has greater purchasing power.

Let's talk about the return on investment. If the funds we've contributed to Social Security over the years had been invested differently, many of us might have seen much higher returns. Private investment in stocks, real estate, or other financial instruments often yields better outcomes than the current Social Security system. This is particularly true in dynamic, emerging markets where growth potential is higher.

Escaping the matrix isn't just about finances; it's about quality of life. In many expat-friendly countries, you'll find communities that welcome foreigners, excellent healthcare services, and a pace of life that allows you to enjoy your retirement years rather than just endure them. Countries like Costa Rica, Portugal, and the Dominican Republic offer vibrant cultures, beautiful landscapes, and living costs that are much lower than in the U.S.

When you choose to escape the matrix, you're making a conscious decision to live life on your own terms. You're opting for a life that's rich in experiences, freedom, and security. It's about recognizing that the world is vast and full of opportunities waiting to be explored.

"We're global now." This simple phrase captures the spirit of this new lifestyle. It's a reminder that we are not confined by borders or traditional expectations. We have the power to redefine what it means to live a fulfilling and secure life. By embracing the idea of escaping the matrix, we open ourselves up to a world of possibilities, ensuring that our best years are truly ahead of us.

Why This Guide is Relevant Today

Ladies and gentlemen, let's take a moment to talk about why a guide like "Escaping the Matrix" is not just relevant but essential in today's world. We are living in times that are, to put it mildly, a bit of a hot mess. Let's break it down:

The State of the Union

Folks, I love my country, I'm a true blue American, but the dream we've heard about since childhood is looking more and more like a fever dream these days. Economic instability, rising costs of living, and a political landscape that's more divided than a Thanksgiving dinner after discussing politics. Many Americans are finding it harder to get ahead, despite working longer hours and taking on more debt. The promise of working hard and retiring comfortably is slipping out of reach for many. It's like running on a treadmill that's set to incline—no matter how fast you go, you're not getting anywhere.

The State of the World

Globally, we're seeing seismic shifts. Geopolitical tensions are rising, and wars and conflicts seem to be ever-present. From the ongoing strife in the Middle East to the geopolitical chess game between major powers, the world is feeling less stable. It's like living next to a volcano—you never know when it's going to erupt, but you know it's coming.

Global Finance

Let's talk money. Inflation is creeping up, interest rates are fluctuating like a rollercoaster, and the gap between the rich and the poor is widening faster than a politician's promises during an election year. For many, the financial future looks uncertain. Your hard-earned savings are losing value, and traditional investments aren't providing the security they once did. It's no wonder people are looking for new ways to make their money work harder for them.

Social Injustice and the "R" Word

We've made strides, but let's be real—racism and social injustice are still deeply rooted issues. Whether it's police brutality, systemic inequality, or everyday discrimination, many people are feeling disillusioned and disenfranchised. It's exhausting to keep fighting the same battles and seeing little change. People are yearning for places where they can live without fear, where they're treated with respect and dignity.

War

Wars and conflicts aren't just historical events—they're current realities. From the war in Ukraine to ongoing conflicts in Africa and the Middle East, the world feels like it's constantly on edge. These conflicts disrupt lives, economies, and futures. People are searching for stability and peace, a place where the sound of bombs is replaced by the sound of waves crashing on peacefully on a beautiful shore. I know for certain I was.

Global Warming

Climate change is no longer a distant threat—it's here. Wildfires, hurricanes, rising sea levels, and unpredictable weather patterns are becoming the norm. It's like Mother Nature is having a midlife crisis, and we're all caught in the fallout. People are looking for places where they can escape the worst effects of climate change, where the environment is still relatively pristine and sustainable living is possible.

Health and Well-being

The COVID-19 pandemic has shown us how fragile our health systems can be. It's highlighted the importance of access to quality healthcare and the need for environments that support physical and mental well-being. People are prioritizing their health more than ever and seeking places that offer better healthcare services and a healthier lifestyle.

With all these factors, it's no wonder that people are considering the idea of escaping the matrix. This guide is your blueprint for navigating this chaotic world and finding a better way to live. It's about leveraging your resources in smarter ways, exploring new opportunities abroad, and creating a life that's not just about survival but about thriving.

Imagine a life where your dollar goes further, where the political climate isn't a constant stressor, and where you can live in harmony with the environment. Imagine a life where you're not just existing but truly living—embracing new cultures, forming new relationships, and finding peace and fulfillment.

So, as we look at the state of America and the world today, it's clear that a guide like this is not just relevant—it's crucial. It's time to think beyond borders, beyond conventional wisdom, and beyond the matrix.

Creating a Stable Base in Your Home Country

Alright folks, let's get down to brass tacks. Before you can start dreaming of sunny beaches, exotic locales, and living your best life abroad, you've got to make sure your foundation is rock solid. Think of this like building a house: if the foundation is shaky, the whole structure is at risk. The same goes for your life. Before you can escape the matrix and embark on this grand adventure, you need to create a stable base in your home country.

Creating a stable base means getting your ducks in a row. It's about ensuring that your financial situation is secure, your personal affairs are in order, and you have a strong support network. This chapter is your guide to laying that groundwork. We'll cover everything from financial planning to maintaining essential relationships, because let's face it, you're going to need a sturdy safety net when you take that leap into the unknown.

Now, I know some of you might be thinking, "DuRon, I'm ready to get out of here now! Why can't I just pack my bags and go?" Believe me, I get it. The urge to escape the daily grind is strong. But trust me on this one—taking the time to prepare now will pay off in spades later. You don't want to find yourself in a foreign country without a backup plan, scrambling to fix things you could have sorted out back home. It's like trying to parachute out of a plane without checking if the chute is packed correctly. Not a good idea, right?

So, let's dive in. We'll start by assessing your current situation and ensuring you have a clear picture of where you stand. Then, we'll move on to financial stability—how to budget, save, and plan for your future abroad. We'll talk about building and maintaining a support network, because having people you can rely on is crucial, whether you're at home or halfway around the world. And finally, we'll cover how to maintain essential relationships and commitments, ensuring you have a lifeline back home.

By the end of this chapter, you'll have a solid foundation in place, ready to support your journey towards escaping the matrix and creating a new life in style. So let's roll up our sleeves and get to work. Remember, a strong base at home sets the stage for an incredible adventure abroad.

Assessing Your Current Situation

Alright, let's start with a reality check. Before you can dream of palm trees and piña coladas, you need to take a good, hard look at where you stand right now. This isn't about judging yourself—it's about understanding your starting point so you can plan your journey effectively. Think of it like setting a GPS: you need to know your current location before you can navigate to your destination.

1. Financial Health

First up, let's talk money. Financial stability is the cornerstone of any successful move abroad. Here's what you need to do:

- Income and Expenses: Take a close look at your income and expenses. Are you living paycheck to paycheck, or do you have a comfortable cushion? Track your spending for a month to see where your money is going. You might be surprised at how those little expenses add up.

- Savings: How much do you have saved up? This isn't just about your emergency fund, though that's crucial too. You need to have enough savings to cover the costs of moving and to support yourself while you settle into your new home.

- Debt: What's your debt situation? Credit cards, student loans, mortgages—list them all. Moving abroad doesn't mean you can run away from your debts. You need a plan to manage or eliminate them.

- Investments: Take stock of your investments. Do you have stocks, bonds, retirement accounts? Knowing what you have and how accessible it is will help you plan your finances better.

2. Personal Affair

Next, let's talk about the personal stuff. These are the things that keep your life running smoothly and give you peace of mind.

- Legal Documents: Make sure all your legal documents are up to date. This includes your passport, driver's license, social security card, birth certificate, and any other important papers. You'll need these for everything from getting a visa to opening a bank account abroad.

- Health: Get a comprehensive health check-up. Make sure you're in good health and have a plan for managing any ongoing health issues. Also, ensure your health insurance is up to date and consider how you'll handle medical coverage when you move.

- Insurance: Review all your insurance policies—health, life, home, auto. Make sure they're adequate and consider what adjustments you might need to make when you move.

3. Relationships and Support Network:

Having a strong support network is crucial, especially when you're making a big life change like moving abroad.

- Family and Friends: Take stock of your relationships. Who can you rely on for support? Make sure you have a plan to stay connected with loved ones back home. Technology makes this easier than ever, so set up regular check-ins.

- Professional Network: Your professional connections can be invaluable. Whether it's for advice, opportunities, or just moral support, make sure you maintain these relationships.

4. Emotional Readiness:

Last but definitely not least, you need to assess your emotional readiness for this move.

- Motivation: Why do you want to move abroad? Be clear about your motivations and goals. This will help keep you focused and driven when the going gets tough.

- Resilience: Moving abroad can be stressful and challenging. Assess your resilience and adaptability. Are you ready to handle the ups and downs that come with such a big change?

- Support: Do you have the emotional support you need? Whether it's a therapist, a mentor, or a trusted friend, having someone to talk to can make a big difference.

By thoroughly assessing your current situation, you're setting yourself up for success. You'll have a clear picture of where you are and what you need to do to prepare for your new life abroad. So, grab a notebook, make those lists, and let's get started. A stable base at home is the first step to creating an extraordinary life beyond the matrix.

Financial Stability and Planning

Now that you've assessed your current financial situation, it's time to focus on building stability and creating a solid plan. Financial stability is the cornerstone of your journey to escaping the matrix. Without it, your dream of living abroad can quickly turn into a nightmare. So let's dive into how you can achieve financial stability and create a plan that sets you up for success.

1. Budgeting

Creating and sticking to a budget is fundamental. A well-planned budget helps you control your spending, save more effectively, and avoid unnecessary debt.

Steps to Create a Budget:

- Track Your Expenses: Use the information from your financial assessment to list all your monthly expenses.
    - Categorize Your Spending: Divide your expenses into categories such as housing, utilities, food, transportation, entertainment, and savings.
    - Set Spending Limits: Assign a spending limit to each category based on your income and financial goals.
    - Monitor and Adjust: Regularly review your budget to see where you might need to adjust your spending. Be flexible and realistic.

Pro Tip: Use budgeting apps like Mint, YNAB (You Need A Budget), or even a simple spreadsheet to help you stay on track.

2. Building an Emergency Fund

An emergency fund is your financial safety net. It protects you against unexpected expenses like medical emergencies, car repairs, or sudden job loss.

How to Build Your Emergency Fund:

- Set a Target Amount: Aim to save at least 3-6 months' worth of living expenses.
    - Automate Savings: Set up automatic transfers from your checking account to your savings account. Even small, regular

contributions add up over time.

- Keep it Accessible: Your emergency fund should be easily accessible in a high-yield savings account, but not so accessible that you're tempted to dip into it for non-emergencies.

3. Managing Debt

Debt can be a significant barrier to financial stability. Prioritizing debt repayment can help you achieve greater financial freedom.

Strategies for Managing Debt:

- List Your Debts: Include all debts from credit cards, student loans, car loans, mortgages, etc., along with their interest rates.
    - Choose a Repayment Strategy:
    - Avalanche Method: Pay off debts with the highest interest rates first.
    - Snowball Method: Pay off the smallest debts first to build momentum.
    - Consolidate or Refinance: Look into consolidating your debts or refinancing to lower your interest rates and monthly payments.
    - Negotiate: Don't be afraid to negotiate with creditors for better terms or seek assistance programs if needed.

4. Saving and Investing

Saving and investing are crucial for building long-term wealth and achieving your financial goals.

Saving:

- Set Clear Goals: Define what you're saving for—whether it's for your move abroad, retirement, a new home, or an emergency fund.
    - Automate Savings: Automate contributions to your savings accounts to ensure consistency.
    - High-Yield Accounts: Use high-yield savings accounts to maximize your interest earnings.

Investing:

- Diversify: Spread your investments across different asset classes to reduce risk. Consider stocks, bonds, mutual funds, real estate, and more.
    - Retirement Accounts: Maximize contributions to retirement accounts like 401(k)s, IRAs, or Roth IRAs. Take advantage of employer matching if available.
    - Seek Professional Advice: If you're unsure about investing, consult with a financial advisor to create a strategy that aligns with your goals.

5. Planning for the Move

Moving abroad requires careful financial planning. Consider the costs involved and how you'll manage your finances in a new country.

Costs to Consider:

- Moving Expenses: Shipping belongings, travel costs, temporary accommodations.

- Visa and Legal Fees: Application fees, legal consultations, residency permits.

- Initial Living Expenses: Rent, utilities, groceries, transportation until you're settled.

- Health Insurance: Coverage for medical expenses in your new country.

- Emergency Fund: Ensure your emergency fund is sufficient to cover unexpected costs during the transition.

Financial Planning Tips:

- Research Cost of Living: Understand the cost of living in your destination country to budget accurately.

- Open International Accounts: Consider opening a bank account in your destination country to facilitate easier transactions.

- Currency Exchange: Be mindful of currency exchange rates and how they impact your budget. Use services that offer favorable rates.

- Tax Implications: Consult with a tax professional to understand the tax implications of living abroad. Ensure you comply with both your home country and destination country's tax laws.

By focusing on financial stability and planning, you're setting yourself up for a smooth transition and a successful life abroad. Remember, the goal is not just to survive but to thrive in your new environment. With a solid financial foundation, you can confidently take the leap and start living the life you've always dreamed of. So, let's get those finances in order and make your escape from the matrix a reality!

Building a Support Network

You've assessed your finances and made a plan. Now it's time to focus on another crucial aspect of your journey: building a support network. Whether you're moving to a new city or a new country, having a strong support system can make all the difference. It's like having a safety net that can catch you when things get tough—and trust me, things will get tough at some point. So, let's dive into how you can build and maintain a support network that will help you thrive.

1. Family and Friends

Your family and friends are your first line of support. These are the people who know you best and have your back no matter what.

Staying Connected:

- Regular Communication: Schedule regular check-ins with your loved ones. This could be through phone calls, video chats, or even old-fashioned letters. The key is consistency.
    - Social Media: Use social media to share your journey and stay updated on what's happening back home. Just remember

to balance screen time with real-life experiences.

- Visits: Plan for visits home or have family and friends come visit you. Having something to look forward to can help mitigate homesickness.

Pro Tip: Create a family group chat or a shared photo album where everyone can stay connected and share updates.

2. Professional Network

Your professional network can provide invaluable support, both before and after your move.

Maintaining Professional Connections:

- LinkedIn: Keep your LinkedIn profile updated and actively engage with your network. Post updates about your move and any professional milestones.
  - Networking Events: Attend virtual or local networking events to meet new contacts and stay connected with existing ones.
  - Professional Organizations: Join professional organizations related to your field in your new country. This can open doors to job opportunities and professional support.

Pro Tip: Reach out to mentors or colleagues who have experience living abroad. Their insights and advice can be incredibly helpful.

3. Expat Communities

Connecting with other expats can provide a sense of belonging and practical support.

Finding Expat Communities:

- Online Forums and Groups: Join online forums, Facebook groups, or websites like Internations.org where expats share experiences and advice.
    - Local Meetups: Look for local expat meetups or social groups in your new country. These can be great for making friends and getting tips on adjusting to your new environment.
    - Language Classes: If you're moving to a non-English speaking country, taking language classes can help you meet other expats and locals alike.

Pro Tip: Participate in community events and volunteer opportunities. This can help you build a diverse network of both expats and locals.

4. Local Connections

Building relationships with locals can help you integrate into your new community and enrich your experience.

Integrating with Locals:

- Learn the Language: Make an effort to learn the local language. This shows respect for the culture and can help you form deeper connections.
    - Cultural Exchange: Participate in cultural exchange programs or events to immerse yourself in the local culture and

meet new people.

- Be Open and Approachable: Show genuine interest in the local way of life. Attend local events, be curious, and strike up conversations.

Pro Tip: Find a local mentor or friend who can help you navigate the nuances of your new environment.

5. Online Resources

Utilize online resources to expand and maintain your support network.

Useful Online Platforms:

- Social Media Groups: Join groups on platforms like Facebook, Reddit, or Instagram that focus on expat life, travel, and your destination country.
- Blogs and Vlogs: Follow blogs or YouTube channels of other expats who share their experiences and tips. This can provide valuable insights and make you feel less alone.
- Webinars and Workshops: Attend online webinars or workshops on topics related to moving abroad, cultural adaptation, and more.

Pro Tip: Create your own blog or social media account to document your journey. Sharing your experiences can help you connect with others and build a supportive community.

6. Emotional Support

Moving to a new country can be an emotional rollercoaster. Having emotional support is crucial for your well-being.

Finding Emotional Support:

- Therapists and Counselors: Consider speaking with a therapist or counselor, especially if you're dealing with significant stress or anxiety. Many offer virtual sessions.
    - Support Groups: Join support groups for expats, either online or in person, where you can share your experiences and hear from others in similar situations.
    - Self-Care: Practice self-care routines to manage stress. This could include meditation, exercise, journaling, or any activity that helps you relax and recharge.

Pro Tip: Don't be afraid to ask for help. Whether it's from a friend, family member, or professional, reaching out can make a big difference.

Building a strong support network is like assembling your very own team of superheroes. Each person brings something unique to the table, and together, they provide the strength and support you need to succeed. As you embark on this journey, remember that you're not alone. With a solid support network, you can face any challenge that comes your way and make the most of your new life abroad. So, start building those connections and get ready to escape the matrix in style!

Maintaining Essential Relationships and Commitments

Moving abroad doesn't mean you're leaving your entire life behind. Your relationships and commitments back home are still vital parts of your life, and maintaining them will help keep you grounded and supported as you navigate your new adventure. Let's explore how to keep these relationships and commitments strong, no matter the distance.

1. Family Ties

Family is your anchor, and staying connected with them can provide emotional stability and support.

Tips for Maintaining Family Relationships:

- Regular Communication: Schedule regular video calls, phone calls, or even written letters. Consistency is key.
  - Share Your Journey: Keep your family updated about your experiences and milestones. Share photos, stories, and even local souvenirs to make them feel part of your new life.
  - Plan Visits: Schedule visits home or invite family members to visit you. This can give you something to look forward to and helps maintain strong bonds.

Pro Tip: Create a family WhatsApp group or use a shared calendar app to keep everyone in the loop about important dates and events.

2. Friendships

Good friends are like stars—they're always there, even when you don't see them. Keeping your friendships strong requires a bit of effort but is well worth it.

Tips for Maintaining Friendships:

- Stay in Touch: Regularly reach out to friends through texts, calls, and social media. Even quick check-ins show you care.
    - Virtual Hangouts: Schedule virtual hangouts or game nights. Technology makes it easy to stay connected despite the distance.
    - Plan Reunions: Organize reunions or trips with friends. Whether it's back home or in a new exciting location, shared experiences strengthen bonds.

Pro Tip: Set up a recurring reminder to check in with friends. It's easy to get caught up in your new life, but regular communication keeps the connection alive.

3. Professional Commitments

Maintaining your professional network and commitments is crucial for career growth and support.

Tips for Maintaining Professional Relationships:

- Update Your Network: Keep your professional network updated about your move and any new opportunities or roles. Use LinkedIn and other professional platforms to stay connected.
    - Virtual Meetings: Schedule virtual coffee chats or meetings with key contacts. Regular communication helps maintain professional relationships.

- Share Your Expertise: Continue to share your expertise and insights through articles, webinars, or social media posts. This keeps you relevant and connected in your field.

Pro Tip: Consider joining professional organizations or groups in your new country. This can help you expand your network while maintaining ties with your existing contacts.

4. Community Involvement

Staying involved in your home community can provide a sense of continuity and fulfillment.

Tips for Maintaining Community Involvement:

- Volunteer Remotely: Many organizations offer remote volunteering opportunities. Find ways to contribute to your community from afar.
- Support Local Causes: Continue to support local causes or charities you care about. Donations, advocacy, and virtual participation can make a difference.
- Stay Informed: Keep up with news and events in your home community. This helps you stay connected and engaged with issues that matter to you.

Pro Tip: Use social media and online platforms to stay connected with community groups and organizations.

5. Financial Commitments

Managing your financial commitments back home is crucial to

avoid any disruptions or complications.

Tips for Managing Financial Commitments:

- Automate Payments: Set up automatic payments for bills, loans, and other recurring expenses to ensure they're paid on time.
    - Monitor Accounts: Regularly check your bank accounts, credit cards, and investments. Use online banking tools to manage your finances efficiently.
    - Consult a Financial Advisor: Consider consulting a financial advisor to help manage your finances across different countries and currencies.

Pro Tip: Keep a list of all your financial commitments and their due dates. This helps you stay organized and avoid any missed payments.

6. Personal Growth and Self-Care

Amidst maintaining relationships and commitments, don't forget to prioritize your personal growth and self-care.

Tips for Personal Growth and Self-Care:

- Set Personal Goals: Establish personal goals for your new life abroad. This could be learning a new language, pursuing a hobby, or focusing on health and fitness.
    - Routine Self-Care: Incorporate self-care routines into your daily life. Exercise, meditation, journaling, and relaxation activities can help you stay balanced.

- Seek Support: If you're feeling overwhelmed, don't hesitate to seek support from a therapist, coach, or support group. Your well-being is paramount.

Pro Tip: Schedule regular "me time" to recharge and reflect. This ensures you stay grounded and focused on your personal well-being.

Maintaining essential relationships and commitments is a balancing act, but it's one that pays off in spades. By staying connected with family, friends, and your professional network, you create a support system that will help you thrive in your new environment. Remember, while you're building a new life abroad, the connections you've made back home are your lifeline. Keep them strong, and you'll always have a solid foundation to rely on as you embark on this exciting journey.

Securing Your Assets Within Your Home Country

Understanding and Organizing Your Resources

Having a clear understanding and organization of your assets is a vital step in preparing for your move abroad. Assets represent your financial health and stability, and they are crucial for making informed decisions and planning your future. Let's break down what you need to do to assess, understand, and organize your assets effectively.

1. Identifying Your Assets

First, you need to identify all your assets. This includes everything you own that has value. Here's a comprehensive list to get you started:

Types of Assets:

- Cash and Bank Accounts: Checking accounts, savings accounts, certificates of deposit (CDs).
    - Investments: Stocks, bonds, mutual funds, retirement accounts (401(k), IRA, etc.), real estate investments.

- Physical Assets: Property (homes, land), vehicles, valuable personal items (jewelry, art, collectibles).
- Business Interests: Ownership in businesses, partnerships, or other commercial ventures.
- Intellectual Property: Patents, trademarks, copyrights.
- Other Assets: Any other valuable items or resources.

Pro Tip: Use a spreadsheet to list all your assets along with their estimated value. This helps you visualize your total wealth and make informed decisions.

2. Valuing Your Assets

Next, you need to determine the current value of each asset. Accurate valuation is crucial for understanding your net worth and planning your finances.

Steps for Valuing Assets:

- Cash and Bank Accounts: Simply note the current balance.
- Investments: Check the current market value of your stocks, bonds, mutual funds, and retirement accounts. Use your financial institution's website or consult with a financial advisor.
- Real Estate: Get a professional appraisal or use online tools to estimate the market value of your properties.
- Vehicles: Use online valuation tools like Kelley Blue Book to determine the current value of your vehicles.
- Personal Items: For valuable items like jewelry or art, consider getting a professional appraisal.
- Business Interests: If you own a business, determine its

value by looking at its financial statements, market position, and future earning potential. Consulting with a business appraiser might be necessary.

- Intellectual Property: Valuing intellectual property can be complex. Consider consulting with an expert in intellectual property valuation.

Pro Tip: Keep documentation for all valuations, such as appraisals, account statements, and receipts. This will be useful for financial planning and in case of disputes or legal matters.

3. Organizing Your Assets

Once you have identified and valued your assets, it's time to organize them. Proper organization ensures that you have easy access to important information and can make efficient decisions.

Organizing Your Assets:

- Create a Digital Inventory: Use a digital spreadsheet or financial software to list all your assets, their values, and relevant details (account numbers, locations, etc.).
- Categorize Assets: Group similar types of assets together (e.g., liquid assets, investments, real estate, personal items). This helps in understanding the composition of your wealth.
- Documentation: Store all relevant documents, such as account statements, property deeds, appraisal reports, and insurance policies, in a secure, accessible location. Consider using a cloud-based service for digital backups.
- Regular Updates: Schedule regular reviews and updates

of your asset inventory. Markets fluctuate, and asset values change, so keep your records current.

Pro Tip: Share your asset inventory with a trusted family member or advisor. This ensures that someone can access important information if you're unavailable.

4. Managing Liabilities

Understanding and organizing your assets also involves managing your liabilities. Liabilities are your debts and obligations, and they directly impact your net worth.

Types of Liabilities:

- Mortgages: Home loans, second mortgages, or equity lines of credit.
   - Loans: Personal loans, auto loans, student loans, business loans.
   - Credit Card Debt: Outstanding balances on credit cards.
   - Other Debts: Any other financial obligations, such as medical bills, legal judgments, or unpaid taxes.

Steps for Managing Liabilities:

- List All Liabilities: Create a comprehensive list of all your debts, including the creditor, current balance, interest rate, and monthly payment.
   - Prioritize Repayment: Focus on paying off high-interest debt first, as it costs you the most in the long run. Consider strategies like debt snowball (paying off small debts first) or

debt avalanche (paying off high-interest debts first).

- Consolidate Debt: If you have multiple high-interest debts, consider consolidating them into a lower-interest loan to simplify payments and reduce interest costs.

- Create a Payment Plan: Develop a clear, realistic plan for paying off your debts. Stick to your budget and adjust as needed to stay on track.

Pro Tip: Consult with a financial advisor if you're struggling with debt. They can provide strategies and resources to help manage and reduce your liabilities.

5. Estate Planning

Estate planning ensures that your assets are distributed according to your wishes and can provide peace of mind for you and your loved ones.

Steps for Estate Planning:

- Create a Will: Outline how you want your assets distributed after your passing. Name an executor to manage your estate.

- Establish Trusts: Consider setting up trusts to manage and protect your assets. Trusts can provide tax benefits and ensure your assets are distributed as intended.

- Designate Beneficiaries: Update beneficiary designations on accounts like life insurance, retirement accounts, and investment accounts.

- Power of Attorney: Assign a power of attorney to manage your affairs if you're unable to do so. This can be a general power of attorney or limited to specific tasks.

- Health Care Directives: Create a living will and designate a health care proxy to make medical decisions on your behalf if you're unable to.

Pro Tip: Review and update your estate plan regularly, especially after major life events like marriage, divorce, the birth of a child, or significant changes in your financial situation.

By understanding and organizing your assets, you're laying a solid foundation for your financial health and future plans. This clarity will help you make informed decisions, manage risks, and ensure that you're well-prepared for your move abroad. It's not just about what you own, but how well you manage and leverage your assets to support your goals and dreams. So take the time to get your financial house in order and move forward with confidence.

Financial Planning and Investment Strategies

Now that you've identified and organized your assets, it's time to dive into financial planning and investment strategies. Proper financial planning and savvy investments are essential for ensuring long-term financial security and achieving your goals abroad. In this section, we'll explore how to create a solid financial plan and make smart investment decisions.

1. Setting Financial Goals

The first step in financial planning is to set clear, achievable goals. Your goals will guide your financial decisions and help you stay focused.

Types of Financial Goals:

- Short-term Goals: These are goals you want to achieve within the next year or two. Examples include saving for a move, paying off a specific debt, or building an emergency fund.
    - Medium-term Goals: These are goals you aim to achieve within the next 3-5 years. Examples include saving for a down payment on a home, investing in a business, or funding a

significant vacation.

- Long-term Goals: These are goals you plan to achieve in 5 years or more. Examples include retirement savings, funding your children's education, or buying a second home.

Setting SMART Goals:

- Specific: Clearly define what you want to achieve.
    - Measurable: Set criteria for measuring progress.
    - Achievable: Ensure your goals are realistic and attainable.
    - Relevant: Make sure your goals align with your broader life objectives.
    - Time-bound: Set a deadline for achieving your goals.

Pro Tip: Write down your financial goals and review them regularly. Adjust them as needed based on changes in your life and financial situation.

2. Creating a Budget

A well-structured budget is the cornerstone of effective financial planning. It helps you manage your income, control expenses, and allocate funds toward your goals.

Steps to Creating a Budget:

- Track Your Income: List all sources of income, including salary, investments, rental income, and any other earnings.
    - List Your Expenses: Categorize your expenses into fixed (rent/mortgage, utilities, loan payments) and variable (groceries, entertainment, dining out). Don't forget to include

savings and investments as part of your expenses.

- Analyze Spending: Review your spending patterns to identify areas where you can cut costs. This will free up more funds for saving and investing.

- Set Spending Limits: Allocate specific amounts for each category of expenses. Ensure you're spending less than you earn.

- Monitor and Adjust: Regularly track your spending against your budget and make adjustments as needed to stay on track.

Pro Tip: Use budgeting apps or financial software to simplify tracking and managing your budget. Many apps offer features like expense categorization and automatic updates.

3. Building an Emergency Fund

An emergency fund is essential for financial security. It acts as a safety net, providing funds for unexpected expenses or financial setbacks.

Steps to Building an Emergency Fund:

- Determine the Amount: Aim to save 3-6 months' worth of living expenses. If you have dependents or a less stable income, consider saving up to 12 months' worth.

- Start Small: Begin by setting aside a small amount each month. Even modest contributions add up over time.

- Automate Savings: Set up automatic transfers to your emergency fund account to ensure consistency.

- Keep it Accessible: Store your emergency fund in a high-yield savings account or a money market account, where it can earn interest but is still easily accessible.

Pro Tip: Avoid using your emergency fund for non-emergencies. This reserve is strictly for unexpected financial needs.

4. Investing Wisely

Investing is crucial for growing your wealth and achieving long-term financial goals. It's important to develop a strategy that aligns with your risk tolerance and objectives.

Basic Principles of Investing:

- Diversification: Spread your investments across different asset classes (stocks, bonds, real estate, etc.) to reduce risk.
    - Risk Tolerance: Understand your risk tolerance and invest accordingly. Higher-risk investments typically offer higher returns but come with greater potential for loss.
    - Time Horizon: Consider your investment time horizon. Long-term investments can weather short-term market volatility.
    - Regular Contributions: Make regular contributions to your investment accounts. Dollar-cost averaging (investing a fixed amount regularly) can reduce the impact of market fluctuations.

Types of Investments:

- Stocks: Investing in individual companies or stock funds. Stocks offer high growth potential but come with higher risk.
    - Bonds: Lending money to governments or corporations in exchange for interest payments. Bonds are generally safer than

stocks but offer lower returns.

- Mutual Funds and ETFs: Pooled investment vehicles that offer diversification. These can be actively or passively managed.

- Real Estate: Investing in property for rental income or appreciation. Real estate can provide steady income and long-term growth.

- Retirement Accounts: Tax-advantaged accounts like 401(k)s or IRAs that help you save for retirement. Take advantage of employer matches if available.

Pro Tip: Consult with a financial advisor to develop a personalized investment strategy. They can provide tailored advice based on your financial situation and goals.

5. Tax Planning

Effective tax planning can help you maximize your income and minimize your tax liability.

Strategies for Tax Planning:

- Understand Tax Laws: Familiarize yourself with the tax laws in both your home country and your destination country. This includes income tax, capital gains tax, and any other applicable taxes.

- Utilize Tax-Advantaged Accounts: Contribute to tax-advantaged accounts like IRAs, 401(k)s, or Health Savings Accounts (HSAs) to reduce your taxable income.

- Keep Records: Maintain thorough records of all your financial transactions, including investments, deductions, and credits. This will simplify tax filing and help you claim all eligible deductions.

- Seek Professional Advice: Consider hiring a tax advisor, especially if you have complex financial situations or are dealing with international taxes.

Pro Tip: Regularly review and adjust your tax strategies based on changes in tax laws and your financial situation.

Financial planning and investment strategies are the bedrock of your financial future, especially as you prepare to move abroad. By setting clear goals, creating a budget, building an emergency fund, investing wisely, and planning for taxes, you can ensure financial stability and growth. This foundation will not only support your new life abroad but also help you navigate any financial challenges that come your way. So, take the time to plan meticulously, invest intelligently, and secure your financial future.

Legal Considerations: Wills, Trusts, and Corporate Structures

As you prepare for your new life abroad, it's essential to address the legal aspects of asset protection and estate planning. Properly structured wills, trusts, and corporate entities can safeguard your assets and ensure your wishes are honored, both in the U.S. and internationally. This section will guide you through the legal considerations you need to keep in mind.

1. U.S.-Based Wills and Trusts

Wills

A will is a legal document that outlines how you want your assets distributed after your death. It's a fundamental part of estate planning and ensures that your wishes are carried out.

Key Elements of a Will:

- Executor: Appoint a trusted individual to manage your estate and ensure your wishes are executed.
    - Beneficiaries: Clearly specify who will inherit your assets, including family members, friends, or charities.
    - Guardianship: If you have minor children, designate a guardian to care for them.
    - Specific Bequests: List any specific items or amounts of money you want to leave to certain individuals.

Pro Tip: Review and update your will regularly, especially after significant life events such as marriage, divorce, the birth of a child, or a major change in financial status.

Trusts

A trust is a legal arrangement where one party (the trustee) holds and manages assets for the benefit of another party (the beneficiary). Trusts can provide tax benefits, protect your assets, and ensure your estate is managed according to your wishes.

Types of Trusts:

- Revocable Living Trust: Allows you to retain control over the trust assets during your lifetime. You can alter or revoke the trust as needed. It helps avoid probate and provides privacy.
    - Irrevocable Trust: Once established, it cannot be altered or revoked. It offers greater asset protection and potential tax benefits.
    - Special Needs Trust: Designed to provide for a disabled beneficiary without affecting their eligibility for government benefits.
    - Charitable Trust: Allows you to donate assets to charity while receiving tax benefits.

Pro Tip: Consult with an estate planning attorney to determine the best type of trust for your needs and ensure it is properly structured.

2. Corporate Structures for Asset Protection

Establishing a corporate structure can provide significant asset protection and tax benefits. Here are some common U.S.-based corporate structures:

Limited Liability Company (LLC)

An LLC is a flexible and straightforward structure that offers liability protection for its owners (members). It can be used to hold various assets, including real estate and investments.

Benefits of an LLC:

- Liability Protection: Members are not personally liable for the company's debts or liabilities.
   - Tax Flexibility: LLCs can choose to be taxed as a sole proprietorship, partnership, S-corporation, or C-corporation.
   - Operational Flexibility: Fewer formalities compared to corporations, with more flexibility in management and operation.

S-Corporation

An S-corporation is a special type of corporation that allows profits, and some losses, to be passed through directly to the owners' personal income without being subject to corporate tax rates.

Benefits of an S-Corporation:

- Pass-Through Taxation: Avoids double taxation by passing income directly to shareholders.
   - Liability Protection: Shareholders are not personally liable for the corporation's debts.
   - Ownership Restrictions: Limited to 100 shareholders, all of whom must be U.S. citizens or residents.

Pro Tip: Work with a corporate attorney and accountant to determine the best corporate structure for your asset protection and tax planning needs.

3. International Options for Corporate Entities and Trust Structures

For those looking to maximize asset protection and tax benefits, establishing international corporate entities and trust structures can be a strategic move. Here are some popular options:

Cayman Islands Corporation

The Cayman Islands is a well-known jurisdiction for establishing offshore corporations due to its favorable tax environment and robust legal framework.

Benefits of a Cayman Islands Corporation:

- No Direct Taxes: No corporate, capital gains, income, or wealth taxes.
    - Privacy: Strong confidentiality laws protect the identity of shareholders and directors.
    - Stability: Politically and economically stable jurisdiction with a well-regulated financial services sector.

Cook Islands Trust

The Cook Islands offers one of the strongest asset protection trust structures available. It is ideal for protecting assets from creditors and legal claims.

Benefits of a Cook Islands Trust:

- Strong Asset Protection: Assets held in a Cook Islands trust are shielded from creditors, legal judgments, and divorce settlements.
    - Confidentiality: High levels of privacy and confidentiality

for settlors and beneficiaries.

   - Flexibility: Trusts can be tailored to meet specific needs and can include a wide range of assets.

Swiss Bank Accounts and Trusts

Switzerland is renowned for its banking secrecy and strong financial services sector. Swiss bank accounts and trusts offer a high level of privacy and asset protection.

Benefits of Swiss Accounts and Trusts:

- Privacy: Swiss banking laws ensure a high level of confidentiality.

   - Stability: Switzerland's political and economic stability makes it a safe haven for assets.

   - Advanced Services: Swiss banks offer sophisticated financial services and asset management.

Pro Tip: Establishing international corporate entities and trusts involves complex legal and tax considerations. Always work with experienced professionals who specialize in international law and finance to ensure compliance and maximize benefits.

By addressing legal considerations such as wills, trusts, and corporate structures, you can protect your assets and ensure your financial legacy is secure. Whether you choose U.S.-based or international options, careful planning and professional advice are essential to navigate the complexities of legal and financial landscapes. With the right strategies in place, you can confidently move forward with your plans to live abroad, knowing your assets are well-protected and your wishes will be honored.

Ensuring Easy Access to Funds Abroad

One of the most crucial aspects of relocating abroad is ensuring that you have easy and reliable access to your funds. Financial difficulties can arise if you don't have a well-established system for accessing your money in a foreign country. This section will highlight the importance of this issue and provide practical strategies to ensure seamless financial access.

1. The Importance of Accessible Funds

Imagine arriving in a new country, ready to start your new life, only to find that you can't access your money. This scenario can turn an exciting adventure into a stressful situation quickly. Easy access to funds is essential for several reasons:

- Daily Expenses: You'll need money for everyday living expenses such as food, transportation, utilities, and entertainment.

- Emergencies: Unexpected situations can arise, requiring immediate access to cash or credit.

- Business Transactions: If you're running a business or managing investments, having quick access to funds is crucial for smooth operations.

- Financial Security: Knowing you can access your money when needed provides peace of mind and financial stability.

2. Opening an International Bank Account

One of the best ways to ensure access to your funds abroad is by opening an international bank account. Many banks offer accounts specifically designed for expatriates, with features that facilitate easy access to money worldwide.

Steps to Open an International Bank Account:

- Research Banks: Look for reputable international banks that offer services in your destination country. Consider banks with a global presence and good customer service.
    - Understand Requirements: Each bank has different requirements for opening an account. Typically, you'll need identification, proof of address, and possibly a reference from your current bank.
    - Choose the Right Account: Select an account that offers low fees for international transactions, online banking, and a network of ATMs in your destination country.
    - Set Up Online Banking: Ensure your account has robust online banking features, allowing you to manage your funds, pay bills, and transfer money easily.

Pro Tip: HSBC, Citibank, and Barclays are examples of banks with strong international services. Check if they have branches or partnerships in your destination country.

3. Maintaining a Home Country Bank Account

Keeping a bank account in your home country can also be beneficial. It allows you to manage ongoing financial commitments back home and provides a fallback option if you encounter issues with your international account.

Benefits of a Home Country Bank Account:

- Flexibility: Maintain the ability to handle transactions in your home country currency.
   - Stability: Use your home account for receiving income, such as pensions or rental income.
   - Emergency Funds: Keep a portion of your savings in your home country as a safety net.

Pro Tip: Notify your home bank of your move to avoid any account freezes due to suspected fraud. Ensure your home account offers international services such as wire transfers and foreign currency exchanges.

4. Using Credit Cards and Debit Cards Abroad

Credit and debit cards are essential tools for managing expenses abroad. However, not all cards are created equal when it comes to international use.

Choosing the Right Cards:

- No Foreign Transaction Fees: Select cards that don't charge extra fees for international purchases.
   - Wide Acceptance: Choose cards from major networks like Visa, MasterCard, or American Express, which are widely

accepted globally.

 - Rewards and Benefits: Opt for cards that offer travel rewards, insurance, and other benefits tailored to expatriates.

Using Cards Safely:

- Notify Your Bank: Inform your bank and card issuers of your travel plans to avoid security blocks.

 - Monitor Statements: Regularly check your account statements for unauthorized transactions.

 - Carry Multiple Cards: Have more than one card in case one is lost, stolen, or not accepted.

Pro Tip: Consider getting a local debit or credit card in your destination country. This can help you avoid exchange rate fees and offer better acceptance for local transactions.

5. International Money Transfers

Transferring money between your home country and your destination can be a critical need. Using the right services can save you money and ensure quick access to your funds.

Money Transfer Options:

- Bank Transfers: Reliable but can be expensive and slow. Check your bank's international transfer fees and processing times.

 - Online Transfer Services: Companies like TransferWise (now Wise), PayPal, and Revolut offer faster and cheaper alternatives for sending money internationally.

 - Currency Exchange Services: Use services that offer competitive exchange rates and low fees.

Pro Tip: Compare fees, exchange rates, and transfer times across different services to find the best option for your needs. Regularly transferring small amounts can also help you avoid large one-time fees.

6. Emergency Access to Funds

In case of emergencies, having a backup plan for accessing funds is crucial. Consider these strategies:

Emergency Strategies:

- Emergency Cash Stash: Keep a small amount of local currency and U.S. dollars hidden in a safe place for immediate access.
   - Trusted Contact: Designate a trusted friend or family member who can quickly transfer money to you if needed.
   - Prepaid Travel Cards: Load money onto a prepaid travel card that you can use like a debit card in emergencies.

Pro Tip: Ensure you know the location of the nearest embassy or consulate, as they can provide assistance in severe emergencies, including financial help.

Ensuring easy access to your funds abroad is a fundamental aspect of your relocation planning. By opening international bank accounts, maintaining home country accounts, using the right credit and debit cards, utilizing efficient money transfer services, and having emergency plans in place, you can avoid financial stress and focus on enjoying your new life abroad. Remember, proper preparation in this area can prevent many potential headaches and provide you with the financial flexibility and security you need.

Researching Expat-Friendly Markets

Identifying Your Needs and Preferences

When considering a move abroad, one of the most critical steps is identifying your unique needs and preferences. This helps ensure your new location aligns with your lifestyle, professional goals, and personal values. Let's dive into how you can assess and prioritize what matters most to you in your new home.

1. Lifestyle Preferences

Climate and Environment:

- Weather: Do you thrive in warm, tropical climates, or do you prefer cooler, temperate zones? Think about how the weather impacts your mood and daily activities.
    - Natural Surroundings: Are you drawn to the beach, mountains, or urban green spaces? The natural environment can significantly influence your quality of life.

Urban vs. Rural:

- City Life: If you enjoy the hustle and bustle, cultural activities, and amenities of city life, look for urban centers.

- Countryside: If you prefer peace, quiet, and a slower pace, rural or suburban areas might be more appealing.

Cultural Amenities:

- Cultural Scene: Consider your interest in local arts, music, theater, and dining. A vibrant cultural scene can enhance your living experience.

- Language: Think about language barriers. Are you open to learning a new language, or do you prefer a place where English is widely spoken?

2. Professional Considerations

Career Opportunities:

- Job Market: Research job opportunities in your field in various countries. Some regions may offer more robust job markets or specific industries.

- Remote Work: If you can work remotely, consider the infrastructure for digital nomads, including internet speed and co-working spaces.

Entrepreneurial Opportunities:

- Starting a Business: Look into the ease of starting and running a business in your potential new home, including legal and regulatory environments.

- Market Demand: Evaluate the demand for your business or services in the local market.

3. Family and Social Needs

Education:

- Schools: If you have children, investigate the quality and type of schools available, including international schools and local education systems.
    - Higher Education: Consider proximity to universities or colleges if you or your family members plan to pursue further education.

Healthcare:

- Medical Facilities: Ensure that quality healthcare services are accessible. Research hospitals, clinics, and healthcare insurance options.
    - Special Needs: If anyone in your family has special medical needs, verify that adequate care and facilities are available.

Community and Social Life:

- Expat Communities: Find out if there are established expatriate communities that can offer support and social opportunities.
    - Local Integration: Consider how easy it will be to integrate into the local community and build a social network.

4. Financial Planning

Cost of Living:

- Budget: Calculate the cost of living in various destinations,

including housing, food, transportation, and entertainment.
   - Income Sources: Ensure your income sources will be sufficient to maintain your desired lifestyle in your new home.

Savings and Investments:

- Financial Stability: Plan for financial stability by understanding local banking systems, investment opportunities, and currency exchange rates.
   - Tax Implications: Research the tax laws in both your home country and potential new country to optimize your financial planning.

5. Personal Safety and Security

Crime Rates:

- Safety: Research the safety and crime rates in potential areas. Feeling secure in your new home is paramount.
   - Precautions: Understand local laws and practices to ensure personal safety and compliance.

Political Stability:

- Stability: Assess the political stability of your potential new home. A stable political environment contributes to overall safety and peace of mind.
   - Legal Environment: Familiarize yourself with local laws and regulations to avoid any legal complications.

6. Environmental Factors

Climate Resilience:

- Natural Disasters: Consider the region's susceptibility to natural disasters like hurricanes, earthquakes, or floods.
   - Climate Change: Evaluate how climate change might impact the area in the future.

Sustainability:

- Eco-Friendliness: If sustainability is important to you, research the environmental policies and practices of potential destinations.

7. Emotional and Cultural Adaptation

Cultural Fit:

- Personal Values: Reflect on how well your personal values align with the cultural norms and societal expectations of your new home.
   - Adaptability: Assess your readiness to adapt to new cultural practices, social norms, and lifestyle adjustments.

Support System:

- Mental Health: Moving abroad can be stressful. Consider the availability of mental health resources and support systems.
   - Social Integration: Think about how easily you can integrate and form meaningful connections in the new community.

Pro Tip: Make a list of your top priorities and rank them.

This can help you focus on what matters most and guide your decision-making process.

Identifying your needs and preferences is a vital step in planning your move abroad. By carefully considering lifestyle preferences, professional opportunities, family needs, financial planning, safety, environmental factors, and cultural adaptation, you can make informed decisions that align with your goals and enhance your overall well-being. Take the time to evaluate what truly matters to you, ensuring a successful and fulfilling transition to your new life.

Resources for Researching Potential Destinations

Choosing the right destination for your new life abroad requires thorough research. Fortunately, there are numerous resources available to help you gather the information you need. This section provides a comprehensive guide to the best tools and platforms for researching potential destinations.

1. Online Expat Communities and Forums

Expat Blogs and Websites:

- InterNations: One of the largest online communities for expatriates, offering country guides, articles, and forums where expats share their experiences.
    - Expatica: Provides news, information, and resources tailored to expatriates living in various countries, particularly in

Europe.

   - ExpatForum: A popular forum where expatriates discuss various aspects of living abroad, including visa processes, housing, and cultural adaptation.

Social Media Groups:

- Facebook Groups: Search for expat groups related to your destination. These groups are often a treasure trove of firsthand experiences and advice.

   - Reddit: Subreddits like r/IWantOut and r/expats provide a platform for asking questions and sharing experiences with a global community.

2. Government and Official Websites

Embassy and Consulate Websites:

- U.S. Department of State: Provides country-specific information, including visa requirements, safety advisories, and local resources for U.S. citizens.

   - Foreign Embassies: Visit the embassy websites of your destination country to get accurate information on visa requirements, residency permits, and legal matters.

Official Tourism Websites:

- National Tourism Boards: These websites offer comprehensive guides to living in their respective countries, covering topics like cost of living, culture, and attractions.

   - Local Government Websites: Provide information on public

services, healthcare, education, and other essential aspects of daily life.

3. Cost of Living Calculators and Financial Tools

Online Calculators:

- Numbeo: A crowd-sourced database that offers detailed cost of living comparisons between cities and countries, including housing, groceries, transportation, and healthcare.
    - Expatistan: Another useful tool for comparing the cost of living between different cities worldwide.

Financial Planning Tools:

- XE Currency Converter: Helps you understand how your home currency converts to the local currency of your potential destination.
    - International Bank Websites: Banks like HSBC and Citibank offer resources and tools for expatriates, including cost of living calculators and financial advice.

4. Real Estate and Housing Platforms

Property Listings:

- Rightmove Overseas: Offers property listings for various countries, helping you get a sense of housing options and prices.
    - International Real Estate Agencies: Websites like Sotheby's International Realty and Century 21 Global provide listings and resources for buying or renting property abroad.

Housing Forums:

- HousingAnywhere: A platform where you can find rental properties and connect with other expats looking for housing.
   - Local Classifieds: Websites like Craigslist or local equivalents often have listings for apartments, houses, and shared accommodations.

5. Travel Guides and Books

Country-Specific Guides:

- Lonely Planet: Offers detailed travel guides that include practical information on living in various countries.
   - Rough Guides: Another excellent resource for comprehensive travel and living information.

Expat Books:

- "The International Living Guide to Retiring Overseas on a Budget" by Suzan Haskins and Dan Prescher: Provides insights and practical advice for living abroad on a budget.
   - "How to Move Abroad and Why It's the Best Thing You'll Do" by Jessica Drucker: A practical guide to moving and living abroad, including tips on finding work, housing, and adjusting to a new culture.

6. Cultural and Language Resources

Cultural Insights:

- Cultural Navigator: Offers insights into cultural norms, business etiquette, and social practices in various countries.
    - Hofstede Insights: Provides detailed analysis of cultural dimensions, helping you understand the cultural differences between your home country and potential destinations.

Language Learning:

- Duolingo: A popular app for learning new languages, ideal for beginners and advanced learners alike.
    - Rosetta Stone: Offers comprehensive language courses that can help you become conversationally proficient before your move.

7. Health and Safety Information

Healthcare Systems:

- World Health Organization (WHO): Provides information on the healthcare systems and health services in different countries.
    - International SOS: Offers health and security advice, medical assistance, and information on healthcare facilities worldwide.

Safety Ratings:

- Global Peace Index: Ranks countries based on their level of peacefulness and safety.
    - Numbeo Crime Index: Provides crime statistics and safety information for various cities and countries.

Pro Tip: Cross-reference information from multiple sources to ensure accuracy and get a well-rounded understanding of your potential destination.

* * *

By utilizing these resources, you can gather comprehensive and reliable information to make informed decisions about your potential new home. Thorough research will not only help you choose the best destination but also prepare you for the challenges and opportunities that come with living abroad. Take advantage of the wealth of information available to ensure a smooth and successful transition to your new life.

Key Factors to Consider

When planning to move abroad, several key factors will significantly impact your experience and quality of life. Evaluating these elements thoroughly will help you make an informed decision and ensure a smooth transition to your new home. Here are the most important factors to consider:

1. Cost of Living

Housing:

- Rent/Purchase Prices: Research the cost of renting or buying property in your chosen destination. This can vary widely between cities and rural areas.

- Utilities: Consider the average cost of utilities, including electricity, water, heating, and internet.

Daily Expenses:

- Groceries and Dining: Compare the cost of groceries and eating out to what you're accustomed to in your home country.

- Transportation: Look into the costs of public transportation, fuel, car maintenance, and any other transportation-related expenses.

- Entertainment and Leisure: Evaluate the cost of entertainment options such as movies, dining, sports, and cultural activities.

Pro Tip: Use tools like Numbeo and Expatistan to compare the cost of living between your current location and potential destinations.

2. Healthcare

Quality of Healthcare:

- Medical Facilities: Research the quality and availability of healthcare facilities in your chosen destination.

- Specialty Care: Ensure that any specific medical needs can be met, especially if you require specialized treatments or medications.

Health Insurance:

- Local Health Insurance: Investigate the local health insurance options available to expatriates and their coverage.
    - International Health Insurance: Consider purchasing international health insurance that provides comprehensive coverage, including emergency evacuation.

Pro Tip: The World Health Organization and International SOS offer detailed information on healthcare systems and facilities around the world.

3. Safety and Security

Crime Rates:

- Safety Statistics: Look into crime rates and safety statistics for your potential new home. Resources like the Global Peace Index and Numbeo Crime Index can be helpful.
    - Neighborhood Safety: Research the safety of specific neighborhoods where you might live.

Political Stability:

- Government Stability: Assess the political stability of the country. Political unrest can impact your safety and quality of life.
    - Regulatory Environment: Understand the local laws and regulations to ensure you remain compliant and avoid legal issues.

Pro Tip: Always stay updated on travel advisories from your home country's government.

4. Education

Schools and Universities:

- Local Schools: If you have children, research the quality and availability of local schools, including international schools.
    - Higher Education: Consider the availability of universities and colleges if higher education is a priority for you or your family.

Educational Standards:

- Curriculum: Evaluate the curriculum offered by local schools and how it compares to your home country's standards.
    - Language of Instruction: Consider the language of instruction and whether your children will need language support.

Pro Tip: Many expat communities and online forums can provide firsthand insights into the local education system.

5. Employment and Business Opportunities

Job Market:

- Employment Opportunities: Research job opportunities in your field in the destination country. Some regions may have a higher demand for your skills than others.
    - Work Permits: Understand the process for obtaining work permits and visas, as well as any restrictions that may apply.

Entrepreneurship:

- Business Environment: Evaluate the ease of starting and running a business, including legal and regulatory requirements.
   - Market Opportunities: Assess the demand for your business or services in the local market.

Pro Tip: Networking with local professionals and joining expatriate business groups can provide valuable insights and connections.

6. Cultural and Social Integration

Language:

- Local Language: Consider your ability to learn and communicate in the local language.
   - Language Support: Look for language classes and support groups that can help you adapt.

Cultural Fit:

- Cultural Norms: Understand the cultural norms and social expectations of your potential new home.
   - Integration: Consider the ease of integrating into the local community and forming social connections.

Pro Tip: Immersing yourself in local cultural activities and traditions can greatly enhance your experience.

7. Infrastructure and Amenities

Transportation:

- Public Transport: Evaluate the availability and efficiency of public transportation options.
    - Roads and Traffic: Consider the condition of roads and the prevalence of traffic congestion.

Utilities and Services:

- Internet and Communication: Check the availability and reliability of internet and communication services.
    - Public Services: Research the quality of public services such as waste management, postal services, and emergency services.

Pro Tip: Visiting your potential new home beforehand can give you a firsthand understanding of the infrastructure and amenities.

8. Legal and Regulatory Environment

Residency and Visas:

- Visa Requirements: Understand the visa and residency requirements for your chosen destination.
    - Legal Residency: Research the process for obtaining legal residency and the associated costs.

Legal Rights:

- Property Ownership: Investigate the laws surrounding property ownership and rental agreements.
    - Employment Laws: Familiarize yourself with local employment laws and workers' rights.

Pro Tip: Consulting with a legal expert or immigration advisor can provide clarity on complex legal matters.

By considering these key factors, you can make a well-informed decision about where to relocate. Each aspect, from cost of living to cultural integration, plays a crucial role in your overall experience and satisfaction in your new home. Take the time to research and prioritize what matters most to you, ensuring a successful and enjoyable transition to living abroad.

Making Initial Contact with Expat Communities

Establishing connections with expatriate communities in your potential new home can be invaluable. These communities provide a wealth of local knowledge, support, and social opportunities, helping you transition smoothly. Here's how to make initial contact and start building your network.

1. Online Forums and Social Media

Expat Forums:

- InterNations: Join InterNations to connect with expatriates in your destination country. The platform offers forums, events, and local groups tailored to various interests.
   - ExpatForum: This site has numerous threads where expats share experiences, advice, and information about living in different countries.

Social Media Groups:

- Facebook: Search for Facebook groups dedicated to expatriates in your desired location. These groups often discuss daily life, offer advice, and organize meetups.

   - Reddit: Subreddits such as r/IWantOut, r/expats, and specific country subreddits are excellent resources for connecting with current expats and asking questions.

Pro Tip: Participate actively in discussions and ask specific questions to get the most relevant advice.

2. Expatriate Associations and Clubs

Local Expat Organizations:

- American and Canadian Clubs: Many cities have clubs specifically for American and Canadian expatriates, providing a familiar cultural environment and social network.

   - International Schools: Schools with large expatriate populations often have parent associations or social groups that welcome new families.

Professional Associations:

- Chambers of Commerce: The local American Chamber of Commerce or other international chambers can be excellent for professional networking.

   - Industry-Specific Groups: Look for professional associations related to your industry, as they often have expatriate members and events.

Pro Tip: Attend events and meetings regularly to build relationships and integrate into the community.

3. Language Classes and Cultural Programs

Language Schools:

- Language Exchange Programs: Participate in language exchange programs to learn the local language while meeting both locals and other expatriates.
    - Cultural Institutes: Institutes like the Alliance Française or the Goethe-Institut often offer language classes and cultural events that attract expatriates.

Community Centers:

- Cultural Centers: Local community or cultural centers frequently host events and activities that provide opportunities to meet people and learn about the local culture.
    - Workshops and Seminars: Look for workshops on topics like local customs, cooking, or history to engage with the community.

Pro Tip: Immersing yourself in local culture and language helps build deeper connections and facilitates a smoother transition.

4. Networking Events and Meetups

Expat Meetups:

- Meetup.com: Use Meetup to find and join groups that match your interests, from hiking clubs to book groups, often with a strong expat presence.
    - InterNations Events: Attend InterNations' regular events,

which are specifically designed for expatriates to socialize and network.

Local Networking Events:

- Business Networking: Attend business networking events and conferences to meet professionals and build a network in your industry.
    - Social Events: Look for local festivals, markets, and social gatherings that welcome newcomers and provide a relaxed environment to meet people.

Pro Tip: Be proactive in attending events and following up with new contacts to build lasting relationships.

5. Volunteering and Community Involvement

Volunteer Opportunities:

- Local Charities: Volunteering with local charities or non-profits is a great way to give back to the community and meet like-minded individuals.
    - International Organizations: Look for opportunities with international organizations that operate in your new country, such as Habitat for Humanity or the Red Cross.

Community Projects:

- Neighborhood Initiatives: Get involved in neighborhood projects or local initiatives to become an active member of your community.

- Educational Programs: Consider volunteering at local schools or community centers, especially if you have specific skills or expertise to offer.

Pro Tip: Volunteering not only helps you integrate but also provides a sense of purpose and belonging in your new environment.

* * *

Making initial contact with expatriate communities is a crucial step in your relocation journey. By leveraging online forums, social media, local organizations, language classes, networking events, and volunteer opportunities, you can build a robust support network that will make your transition smoother and more enjoyable. Engaging with these communities will provide you with practical advice, emotional support, and social connections, helping you settle into your new life with confidence and ease.

Understanding the Legal Landscape

Moving to a new country involves navigating a complex web of legal requirements and regulations. This chapter will guide you through the essential legal considerations, from visa and residency requirements to work permits, tax implications, and understanding the legal systems in your destination country. Properly addressing these issues will ensure a smooth transition and help you avoid potential pitfalls.

Visa and Residency Requirements

Types of Visas

Tourist Visas:

- Short-Term Stay: Often valid for 30-90 days, these visas are ideal for initial visits to explore your destination.
    - Extensions: Some countries allow you to extend tourist visas, but this is usually not a long-term solution.

Work Visas:

- Employer-Sponsored: Typically required if you have a job offer from a company in the destination country.

- Self-Employed/Entrepreneur Visas: Designed for individuals planning to start a business or freelance in the new country.

Student Visas:

- Educational Pursuits: Necessary if you or your dependents plan to study at an educational institution abroad.

- Work Rights: Some student visas allow part-time work to support your studies.

Retirement Visas:

- Retiree Benefits: Countries like Thailand, Mexico, and Portugal offer retirement visas with specific financial requirements.

- Health Insurance: Often required as part of the application process.

Residency Permits

Temporary Residency:

- Initial Step: Usually granted for one to five years, providing time to establish yourself in the country.

- Renewal: Ensure you understand the renewal process and requirements.

Permanent Residency:

- Long-Term Stay: Offers more stability and often includes benefits like access to local healthcare and education.

- Requirements: Vary widely but may include language proficiency, financial stability, and clean criminal records.

Pro Tip: Always check the latest requirements on official government websites or consult with an immigration lawyer to avoid surprises.

Work Permits and Employment Laws

Obtaining a Work Permit

Employer Responsibilities:

- Sponsorship: Your employer may need to sponsor your work permit application.
  - Documentation: Ensure all required documents, such as job contracts and proof of qualifications, are in order.

Self-Employment:

- Freelancing: Some countries allow self-employed individuals to obtain work permits, but requirements can be stringent.
  - Business Registration: You may need to register a local business entity to qualify for a permit.

Pro Tip: Start the work permit application process early to avoid delays that could impact your move.

Employment Laws

Contracts:

- Written Contracts: Ensure you receive a written employment contract outlining job responsibilities, salary, and benefits.
    - Local Standards: Familiarize yourself with local employment standards, such as working hours, overtime, and leave entitlements.

Workers' Rights:

- Minimum Wage: Understand the minimum wage laws and ensure your salary meets or exceeds these standards.
    - Employment Protection: Know your rights regarding termination, redundancy, and workplace safety.

Pro Tip: Joining a local workers' union can provide additional support and information about your rights.

Tax Implications and Strategies

Understanding Tax Obligations

Home Country Taxes:

- Tax Residency: Determine if you will remain a tax resident in your home country and how this affects your obligations.
    - Double Taxation Agreements (DTAs): Check if there is a DTA between your home country and your destination to avoid being taxed twice on the same income.

Foreign Country Taxes:

- Income Tax: Understand the income tax rates and filing

requirements in your new country.

- Wealth and Property Taxes: Research any wealth or property taxes that may apply to your assets abroad.

Pro Tip: Consulting with a tax advisor who specializes in international taxation can help you navigate these complexities.

Tax Strategies

Tax Planning:

- Expat Tax Benefits: Some countries offer tax incentives for expatriates, such as tax holidays or reduced rates.
- Offshore Accounts: Consider the benefits and legalities of holding offshore bank accounts to optimize tax efficiency.

Investments:

- Tax-Efficient Investments: Explore investment options that offer tax benefits in your new country.
- Retirement Funds: Understand how your move affects your retirement savings and whether you can continue contributing to home country accounts.

Pro Tip: Regularly review and update your tax strategy to adapt to changes in tax laws and personal circumstances.

Navigating Legal Systems in Foreign Countries

Understanding Local Laws

Legal Framework:

- Civil vs. Common Law: Know whether your destination follows a civil law or common law system, as this impacts legal processes and rights.
    - Key Regulations: Familiarize yourself with essential regulations, such as property ownership laws, business registration, and consumer rights.

Legal Assistance:

- Hiring a Lawyer: Engaging a local lawyer can provide invaluable guidance on navigating the legal system and ensuring compliance with local laws.
    - Legal Aid: Investigate whether you qualify for legal aid services, which can help reduce costs if legal issues arise.

Pro Tip: Attend local legal workshops or seminars to stay informed about relevant legal changes and practices.

Dispute Resolution

Court System:

- Judicial Structure: Understand the structure of the local court system and the process for resolving disputes.
    - Filing a Case: Know the procedure for filing legal cases and the typical timeline for resolution.

Alternative Dispute Resolution (ADR):

- Mediation and Arbitration: Explore ADR options, such as mediation or arbitration, which can be quicker and less costly than court proceedings.
   - Local ADR Services: Research local organizations that offer ADR services to help resolve disputes amicably.

Pro Tip: Keeping detailed records of all transactions and communications can be crucial in resolving disputes effectively.

* * *

Understanding the legal landscape is crucial for a successful move abroad. From securing the right visa and work permits to navigating tax implications and local laws, being well-informed and prepared can make a significant difference. Take the time to research, consult with professionals, and stay proactive to ensure a smooth and legally sound transition to your new home.

Political Stability and Safety

Embarking on a journey to a new country requires a comprehensive understanding of its political stability and safety landscape. This chapter delves into the essential aspects you need to consider, including evaluating political climates, safety and security considerations, understanding local laws and customs, and utilizing resources to stay informed and connected.

Evaluating Political Climates

When assessing the political climate of a country, it's crucial to understand its historical and current political dynamics. This involves:

Researching Historical Context

Understanding a country's political history can provide insights into its current stability. Look into:

- Historical Conflicts: Wars, revolutions, and significant political changes.

- Political Leadership: Changes in leadership and their impact on the country.

- Government Structure: The type of government and its stability over time.

Monitoring Current Events

Stay updated on current political events through:

- News Outlets: Reputable international and local news sources.

- Government Reports: Statements and reports from official government websites.

- Political Analysis: Insights from political analysts and think tanks.

Evaluating Stability Indicators

Key indicators of political stability include:

- Economic Performance: A stable economy often correlates with political stability.

- Social Unrest: Levels of protests, strikes, and civil unrest.

- Corruption Levels: Transparency International's Corruption Perceptions Index can be a useful resource.

Safety and Security Considerations

Your personal safety is paramount when relocating. Consider the following aspects:

Crime Rates and Types

Understand the prevalent types of crime in the country:

- Violent Crime: Rates of assault, robbery, and other violent crimes.

- Property Crime: Incidence of theft, burglary, and vandalism.

- Organized Crime: Presence of gangs or organized criminal activities.

Health and Medical Services

Evaluate the availability and quality of healthcare services:

- Hospitals and Clinics: Proximity and quality of medical facilities.

- Health Risks: Prevalence of diseases and availability of vaccinations.

- Health Insurance: Accessibility and cost of health insurance for expatriates.

Emergency Services

Ensure you know how to access emergency services:

- Emergency Numbers: Local emergency contact numbers for police, fire, and medical services.

- Response Times: Efficiency and reliability of emergency response services.

Understanding Local Laws and Customs

Adapting to a new legal and cultural environment is crucial for a smooth transition:

Legal System

Familiarize yourself with the legal system:

- Legal Codes: Key laws that impact daily life, such as traffic regulations, property laws, and employment regulations.

- Legal Rights: Your rights as a resident or expatriate.

- Law Enforcement: Structure and role of local law enforcement agencies.

Cultural Norms and Practices

Understanding cultural norms can help avoid misunderstandings:

- Social Etiquette: Accepted behaviors and customs in social interactions.
- Dress Code: Appropriate attire for different settings and occasions.
- Communication Styles: Local communication practices, including body language and formalities.

Religious Practices
Be aware of religious practices and their influence on daily life:
- Religious Holidays: Important religious holidays and their impact on business and daily activities.
- Religious Sensitivities: Respect for religious practices and places of worship.

Resources for Staying Informed and Connected

Utilizing the right resources can help you stay informed and connected:

Government Resources
Leverage resources from your home country and the host country:
- Embassy Websites: Information on safety, security, and consular services.
- Travel Advisories: Official travel advisories and warnings.

News and Information Services
Stay updated with reliable news sources:
- Local News: Newspapers, television, and radio stations.
- International News: Global news networks and online

platforms.

Community Networks
Connect with local and expatriate communities:
- Social Media Groups: Online forums and social media groups for expatriates.
- Local Associations: Community groups and clubs for net-working and support.

Technology and Apps
Utilize technology for safety and information:
- Safety Apps: Mobile apps for emergency alerts and safety information.
- Communication Tools: Apps for staying in touch with family and friends.

By carefully evaluating political climates, prioritizing safety and security, understanding local laws and customs, and leveraging available resources, you can navigate your new environment with confidence and peace of mind. This approach will help ensure a safe and stable experience as you embark on your journey to a new country.

Cultural Adaptation

Adapting to a new culture can be both exhilarating and challenging. It's not just about learning the language or knowing the local customs; it's about immersing yourself in a whole new way of life. This chapter is your guide to understanding cultural differences, learning the language, building relationships with locals, and integrating into your new community. Let's dive in and make this transition as smooth and enriching as possible.

Understanding Cultural Differences

Embracing Diversity

You're stepping into a world that might be vastly different from what you're used to. And that's the beauty of it. Understanding cultural differences means embracing diversity, respecting local traditions, and being open to new perspectives.

Local Customs and Traditions:

- Respecting Traditions: Every culture has its unique set of traditions and customs. Learn about local holidays, festivals, and ceremonies. Participate where you can, and show respect even if you don't fully understand them yet.

- Social Norms: From greeting people to dining etiquette, social norms can vary widely. Observe and follow local practices to show respect and build rapport.

Pro Tip: Don't be afraid to ask questions. Locals often appreciate it when newcomers show genuine interest in their culture.

Avoiding Cultural Missteps

Common Pitfalls:

- Stereotyping: Avoid making assumptions based on stereotypes. Every individual is unique, and it's important to approach each person with an open mind.
- Miscommunication: Language barriers and different communication styles can lead to misunderstandings. Be patient, listen actively, and clarify when needed.

Pro Tip: Humor is universal, but it's also culturally specific. Be mindful of local humor and sensitivities to avoid unintentional offense.

Learning the Language

Importance of Language Skills

Learning the local language is more than just a practical necessity; it's a gateway to deeper cultural understanding and connection.

Everyday Communication:

- Basic Phrases: Start with essential phrases and greetings. Knowing how to say "hello," "please," and "thank you" can go a long way.
    - Conversational Skills: Aim to build your conversational skills over time. Practice regularly, and don't worry about making mistakes – they're part of the learning process.

Pro Tip: Language apps like Duolingo or Rosetta Stone can be great starting points, but nothing beats real-life practice with native speakers.

Language Learning Strategies

Immersive Learning:

- Language Classes: Enroll in language classes. They not only teach you the language but also provide a structured environment to practice.
    - Language Partners: Find a language exchange partner – someone who wants to learn your language in exchange for helping you with theirs.

Daily Practice:

- Media Consumption: Watch local TV shows, listen to radio stations, and read newspapers. This helps with comprehension and familiarizes you with local accents and slang.
    - Labeling: Label items around your home in the new language. This constant exposure helps reinforce vocabulary.

Pro Tip: Don't shy away from using the language in daily interactions. The more you use it, the more confident you'll become.

Building Relationships with Locals

Making Connections

Building meaningful relationships with locals can greatly enhance your experience and help you integrate into the community.

Be Approachable:

- Open Body Language: Smile, make eye contact, and show openness in your body language.
   - Join Local Groups: Participate in local clubs, sports teams, or hobby groups. Shared interests are a great way to connect.

Pro Tip: Volunteering is an excellent way to meet locals and contribute to your new community. It shows that you're invested in being a part of the local fabric.

Navigating Social Interactions

Understanding Social Etiquette:

- Greetings and Gestures: Learn the appropriate ways to greet people. Some cultures value a firm handshake, while others prefer a bow or a kiss on the cheek.
   - Gift-Giving: In some cultures, gift-giving is an important

social ritual. Understand the norms around it, including what types of gifts are appropriate.

Pro Tip: Take cues from locals. Observe how they interact and follow suit. If in doubt, ask for guidance – people are usually happy to explain their customs.

Integrating into the Community

Becoming an Active Participant

Integration is about being an active participant in your new community, not just a passive observer.

Community Events:

- Festivals and Celebrations: Attend local festivals and community celebrations. These events are a window into the heart of the culture.
   - Local Markets: Shop at local markets and interact with vendors. It's a great way to practice the language and get a feel for everyday life.

Pro Tip: Take up a local hobby or sport. Whether it's learning to dance salsa in Latin America or playing cricket in India, participating in local activities helps you feel more at home.

Contributing to the Community

Giving Back:

- Volunteer Work: Offer your time and skills to local organizations. It's a rewarding way to give back and build connections.
   - Community Projects: Get involved in community projects or initiatives. Your unique perspective and skills can be valuable assets.

Pro Tip: Approach integration with humility and respect. You're entering a community with its own history and dynamics. Show that you're there to learn and contribute, not to impose your own ways.

* * *

Cultural adaptation is a journey. It's about stepping out of your comfort zone, embracing the unknown, and finding a new rhythm in a different environment. By understanding cultural differences, learning the language, building relationships with locals, and actively participating in the community, you'll not only adapt but thrive in your new home. This chapter has given you the tools to start this journey with confidence and enthusiasm. Remember, it's not just about surviving – it's about creating a life that's rich, fulfilling, and connected to the world around you.

Financial Management Abroad

Navigating the financial landscape in a new country can be as thrilling as it is daunting. This chapter will equip you with the tools and knowledge to manage your finances effectively abroad. From banking and financial services to budgeting for expat life, we'll cover everything you need to ensure financial stability and growth in your new home. Let's dive in and master your money on foreign soil.

Banking and Financial Services

Setting Up Bank Accounts

Opening a local bank account is one of the first steps you should take after moving. It will simplify your financial transactions, from paying bills to receiving income.

Choosing the Right Bank:

- Local vs. International Banks: International banks may offer familiarity and ease of transferring funds between countries, while local banks can provide better access to local financial services and lower fees.

- Account Types: Understand the different types of accounts available, such as savings, checking, and fixed deposits, and choose what best suits your needs.

Pro Tip: Some countries have strict requirements for opening a bank account, such as proof of residency or a local address. Make sure you have all necessary documentation in order.

Online and Mobile Banking

Digital Convenience:

- Mobile Apps: Many banks offer comprehensive mobile apps that allow you to manage your finances on the go. Look for features like bill pay, fund transfers, and real-time transaction alerts.
   - Online Banking: Ensure your bank provides a robust online banking platform for easy access to your accounts and financial services.

Pro Tip: Prioritize banks that offer 24/7 customer support and secure online platforms to safeguard your financial information.

Managing Currency Exchange and Transfer Fees

Currency Exchange

Dealing with currency exchange can significantly impact your finances. Understanding the best ways to handle it can save you money and hassle.

Exchange Rates:

- Monitoring Rates: Keep an eye on exchange rates and try to transfer money when rates are favorable. Tools like XE or OANDA can help you track rates.
   - Exchange Services: Compare rates and fees from different exchange services, including banks, online platforms, and local exchange bureaus.

Pro Tip: Avoid airport exchange counters, as they often offer less favorable rates.

Transfer Fees

Transferring money across borders can be expensive if you're not careful. Knowing how to minimize fees is crucial.

Transfer Methods:

- Bank Transfers: While secure, bank transfers can be costly due to high fees and less favorable exchange rates.
   - Online Transfer Services: Services like TransferWise (now Wise), Revolut, and PayPal often offer lower fees and better rates.
   - Cryptocurrency Transfers: For tech-savvy individuals, cryptocurrency can be a fast and cost-effective way to transfer funds internationally, though it comes with its own set of risks and regulations.

Pro Tip: Plan your transfers in advance to take advantage of the best rates and lowest fees. Avoid urgent transfers which can be more expensive.

Budgeting for Expat Life

Creating a Realistic Budget

Living abroad can come with unexpected costs. Having a well-thought-out budget helps you manage your expenses and avoid financial stress.

Monthly Expenses:

- Housing: Rent or mortgage payments, utilities, and maintenance costs. Consider whether you'll be living in the city center or a more affordable suburban area.
    - Transportation: Costs for public transport, car ownership, and fuel. Don't forget insurance and potential import taxes if you bring your own vehicle.
    - Food and Groceries: Eating out vs. cooking at home can have a big impact on your budget. Local markets might offer fresher and cheaper options than supermarkets.

Pro Tip: Track your spending for the first few months to understand your actual expenses and adjust your budget accordingly.

Emergency Fund

Financial Safety Net:

- Savings: Aim to set aside three to six months' worth of living expenses. This fund can cover unexpected costs like medical emergencies or sudden job loss.

   - Access: Ensure your emergency fund is easily accessible but kept separate from your regular spending accounts to avoid temptation.

Pro Tip: Regularly review and adjust your emergency fund based on changes in your financial situation and living costs.

Building Wealth in a Foreign Country

Investment Opportunities

Living abroad opens up new avenues for investment, from local real estate to international markets.

Local Investments:

- Real Estate: Investing in local property can provide rental income and capital appreciation. Understand the local market and legal requirements before purchasing.
   - Stocks and Bonds: Explore the local stock market and government bonds. These can offer growth opportunities and diversify your investment portfolio.

Pro Tip: Consult with a local financial advisor who understands the investment landscape and can provide tailored advice.

Retirement Planning

Future Security:

- Pension Plans: Check if you can contribute to your home country's pension plan while abroad. Alternatively, explore local pension schemes.

- Savings Accounts: Consider setting up a high-yield savings account or an investment account dedicated to your retirement fund.

Pro Tip: Regularly review your retirement plan to ensure it aligns with your long-term financial goals and adjust for any changes in your personal or financial situation.

* * *

Financial management abroad is about more than just handling your day-to-day expenses. It's about creating a stable financial foundation, minimizing costs, planning for the future, and building wealth in your new environment. By setting up the right banking services, managing currency exchanges and transfer fees smartly, budgeting effectively, and exploring investment opportunities, you'll be well on your way to achieving financial stability and success in your new home. Remember, sound financial management is key to making your expat life not only viable but thriving.

Healthcare and Insurance

Navigating healthcare in a new country can be one of the most crucial aspects of your relocation. Ensuring you have access to quality medical care and understanding your health insurance options will provide peace of mind and security. This chapter will guide you through the essentials of the local healthcare system, health insurance options for expats, accessing quality medical care, and preventative health measures and resources. Let's dive into ensuring your health and well-being in your new home.

Understanding the Local Healthcare System

Public vs. Private Healthcare

Healthcare systems vary significantly from country to country, and understanding the distinction between public and private healthcare is essential.

Public Healthcare:

- Availability: Many countries offer public healthcare systems funded by taxes, providing free or low-cost medical services to residents.

- Quality and Access: While public healthcare can be of high quality, it often involves longer wait times and may have limited resources.

Private Healthcare:

- Access: Private healthcare offers quicker access to medical services and often features more modern facilities.
- Cost: These services come at a higher cost, and having adequate insurance coverage is crucial to avoid out-of-pocket expenses.

Pro Tip: Research the healthcare system in your destination country before you move to understand what's available and what you'll need to supplement with private care.

Health Insurance Options for Expats

Types of Health Insurance

Choosing the right health insurance is critical for ensuring you can access medical care without financial strain.

Local Health Insurance:

- Eligibility: Some countries require expats to enroll in their national health insurance system as part of the residency process.
- Coverage: Local insurance often covers a range of services, including doctor visits, hospitalization, and emergency care,

but may exclude pre-existing conditions.

International Health Insurance:

- Comprehensive Coverage: International health insurance plans are designed for expats and provide coverage across multiple countries, including your home country.
    - Flexibility: These plans typically offer more comprehensive benefits, including coverage for pre-existing conditions, evacuation services, and global medical networks.

Pro Tip: Compare various health insurance plans to find one that best suits your needs and budget. Look for plans that offer flexibility and comprehensive coverage.

Selecting the Right Plan

Coverage Needs:

- Medical History: Consider your medical history and any pre-existing conditions when selecting a plan. Ensure the plan covers regular treatments and potential emergencies.
    - Family Coverage: If you're moving with your family, choose a plan that covers everyone, including maternity and pediatric care if needed.

Budget Considerations:

- Premiums vs. Out-of-Pocket Costs: Balance the cost of premiums with potential out-of-pocket expenses. A plan with lower premiums might have higher co-pays and deductibles.

Pro Tip: Consult with an insurance broker who specializes in expat health insurance to get personalized advice and find the best plan for your situation.

Accessing Quality Medical Care

Finding Medical Providers

Ensuring access to quality medical care involves finding reputable healthcare providers and facilities.

Local Recommendations:

- Expats and Locals: Seek recommendations from fellow expats and locals. They can provide insights into the best doctors, clinics, and hospitals.
   - Embassies: Some embassies maintain lists of recommended medical providers and can offer guidance.

Pro Tip: Join local expat forums and social media groups to get firsthand recommendations and reviews of medical providers.

Emergency Medical Services

Emergency Numbers:

- Know the Numbers: Familiarize yourself with the local emergency numbers for ambulance, fire, and police services. Keep these numbers accessible at all times.
   - Local Hospitals: Identify the nearest hospitals and emergency rooms. Know the fastest route to these facilities from

your home.

Pro Tip: Carry a card with your blood type, allergies, and any chronic conditions in the local language. This information can be critical in an emergency.

Preventative Health Measures and Resources

Routine Health Checks

Preventative health care is essential to maintain your well-being and catch potential issues early.

Regular Check-Ups:

- Annual Exams: Schedule regular health check-ups and screenings. Many health issues can be managed more effectively if detected early.
   - Vaccinations: Ensure you and your family are up-to-date on vaccinations. Check if any additional vaccines are recommended for your new country.

Pro Tip: Use local healthcare facilities for routine checks to familiarize yourself with the system and build relationships with medical providers.

Healthy Living Resources

Local Health Initiatives:

- Fitness Centers: Join local gyms, yoga studios, or sports

clubs to stay active. Many communities have public parks with exercise equipment and walking trails.

- Healthy Eating: Explore local markets for fresh produce and learn about traditional foods that contribute to a healthy diet.

Pro Tip: Engage in local health initiatives and community events to stay informed about available resources and health programs.

* * *

Healthcare and insurance are foundational to your successful relocation. Understanding the local healthcare system, selecting the right health insurance, ensuring access to quality medical care, and adopting preventative health measures will help you maintain your health and well-being abroad. By taking proactive steps, you can enjoy peace of mind and focus on the many exciting aspects of your new life. Stay healthy, stay informed, and make the most of your expat journey.

Education and Family Considerations

Alright, folks, let's talk about something close to all our hearts—family. When you're planning a move abroad, making sure your family is taken care of, especially the little ones, is paramount. We're diving into education options for your kids, supporting your family's adaptation, balancing family and personal goals, and tackling the challenges that come your way. Let's break it down and make sure your family thrives in your new home.

Education Options for Children

Local Schools vs. International Schools

First up, the big question: Where are the kids going to school? Choosing the right educational environment is crucial for their development and well-being.

Local Schools:

- Immersion Experience: Sending your kids to a local school can be a great way for them to learn the language and integrate into the culture.
    - Cost: Generally more affordable than international schools,

but the quality can vary.

International Schools:

- Familiar Curriculum: These schools often follow curricula from the U.S., U.K., or other Western countries, making the transition smoother for your kids.
    - Community: A diverse student body means your kids will meet peers from all over the world, creating a rich, multicultural environment.

Pro Tip: Visit schools, talk to administrators, and if possible, connect with other expat parents to get the inside scoop on what's best for your kids.

Supporting Your Family's Adaptation

Helping Everyone Settle In

Moving abroad is a big adjustment for everyone. Here's how to make sure your family transitions smoothly.

Cultural Adjustment:

- Learn Together: Take language classes as a family. It's a fun way to bond and integrate into your new community.
    - Explore Together: Make it a point to explore your new surroundings together. Visit local markets, landmarks, and cultural sites.

Pro Tip: Encourage each family member to pursue their inter–

ests and hobbies. It's a great way for everyone to make new friends and feel at home.

Emotional Support

Relocating can be an emotional rollercoaster. Providing emotional support is key to a smooth transition.

Open Communication:

- Check-In Regularly: Have regular family meetings to discuss how everyone is feeling. Make sure everyone feels heard and supported.
   - Stay Positive: Focus on the positives of your new life while acknowledging the challenges.

Pro Tip: Keep a family journal where everyone can write down their experiences and feelings. It's a great way to process the transition together.

Balancing Family and Personal Goals

Finding Harmony

It's important to strike a balance between your personal aspirations and family responsibilities.

Set Clear Goals:

- Individual Goals: Make sure everyone has personal goals they're working towards, whether it's learning the language,

making new friends, or pursuing a hobby.
   - Family Goals: Set family goals, like traveling to different parts of your new country, attending cultural events, or achieving milestones together.

Pro Tip: Schedule regular family activities that align with everyone's interests. It ensures quality time together and supports individual passions.

Addressing Challenges and Seeking Support

Navigating Difficulties

Challenges are part of the journey, but with the right approach, you can overcome them.

Common Challenges:

- Homesickness: Feeling homesick is normal. Stay connected with loved ones back home through regular calls and visits if possible.
   - Cultural Misunderstandings: Misunderstandings can happen. Approach them with patience and a sense of humor.

Pro Tip: Join expat groups and local community organizations. They offer support, resources, and a network of people who understand what you're going through.

Professional Support

Sometimes, you might need professional help to navigate more significant challenges.

Seeking Help:

- Counseling Services: Don't hesitate to seek counseling or therapy if someone in the family is struggling to adapt.
   - Educational Support: If your child is having difficulty at school, look into tutoring or special educational programs.

Pro Tip: Many international schools offer counseling and support services for students and families. Take advantage of these resources.

* * *

Education and family considerations are at the heart of a successful move abroad. By exploring education options, supporting your family's adaptation, balancing personal and family goals, and addressing challenges head-on, you'll create a nurturing and fulfilling environment for everyone. This chapter equips you with the tools to ensure your family not only survives but thrives in your new adventure. Remember, it's all about building a life where everyone feels at home, connected, and supported. Let's make sure your family's journey is as enriching and joyful as possible.

Our Favorite Countries for Expat Escapism

Welcome to Chapter 10, where we get down to the nitty-gritty of choosing your new home away from home. We're going global, folks. We're diving into the Dominican Republic, Ghana, Spain, Mexico, Costa Rica, Portugal, Italy, Colombia, Ireland, and Turkey. Each of these countries offers a unique blend of legal, political, and cultural landscapes that could be the perfect fit for your new life.

Picture this: you're sipping coffee on a terrace in Colombia, watching the sun rise over the mountains. Or maybe you're strolling through the historic streets of Rome, marveling at centuries-old architecture. Perhaps you're relaxing on a pristine beach in the Dominican Republic, enjoying the vibrant culture and laid-back lifestyle. Sounds dreamy, right? But it's not just about the scenery; it's about finding a place where you can truly thrive.

In this chapter, we're going to break down what makes each of these ten countries a viable option for expats. We'll delve into the details of their legal systems, political stability, and cultural richness. You'll hear success stories from expats who've made the leap and never looked back. Plus, we'll provide country-specific tips and advice to help you navigate your new surroundings with ease.

First up, we'll explore the legal landscape of each country. What are the visa and residency requirements? How do work permits and employment laws operate? We'll also look at the political climate, because stability is key when choosing a new home. Lastly, we'll dive into the cultural nuances that make each country unique. Understanding these differences can help you integrate more smoothly and fully appreciate your new environment.

Hearing from those who've walked the path before you can be incredibly inspiring and insightful. We've gathered stories from expats who've successfully transitioned to life in these countries. They'll share their challenges, triumphs, and the lessons they've learned along the way. These narratives provide real-world perspectives that can help you anticipate and navigate your own journey.

Each country has its own quirks and charm. We'll provide practical tips on everything from finding housing and setting up utilities to understanding local customs and etiquette. Whether it's negotiating the property market in Spain or understanding the healthcare system in Costa Rica, these tips will equip you with the knowledge you need to settle in with confidence.

Finally, we'll point you towards additional resources to help you continue your research and make connections in your chosen country. From online forums and expat groups to government websites and local services, these resources are invaluable for ongoing support and information.

This chapter is your roadmap to making an informed decision about where to start your new life. Each of these ten countries offers something unique, and by the end of this chapter, you'll have a clear idea of which one resonates most with your dreams and goals. Let's embark on this journey together and find the perfect destination for your next great adventure.

Dominican Republic: Our Favorite Destination

Mi Gente, today we journey to a land of stunning landscapes, rich culture, and warm hospitality—the Dominican Republic. Known affectionately as "the DR," this Caribbean jewel is not just a destination; it's a place where dreams come alive and new beginnings flourish. Whether you're drawn to its sandy beaches, lush mountains, or bustling city life, the DR has something for everyone. So, let's dive deep into what makes this nation an ideal haven for those looking to escape the matrix and build a new life abroad.

Legal Landscape

Visa and Residency Requirements

Understanding the visa and residency requirements is crucial for a smooth transition to your new life in the DR. Let's break it down:

Tourist Visa:

- Duration: Visitors from many countries, including the U.S.,

Canada, and EU nations, can enter the DR without a visa for up to 30 days.

- Extension: If you wish to stay longer, you can extend your tourist visa for an additional 60 days by visiting the immigration office in Santo Domingo.

Residency Visa:

- Types: The DR offers temporary and permanent residency options.
- Temporary Residency: Ideal for those planning to stay more than 60 days but less than a year. Applications must be submitted at a Dominican consulate in your home country.
- Permanent Residency: After holding temporary residency for five years, you can apply for permanent residency. Immediate permanent residency is available under specific conditions, such as retirement or substantial investment.

Application Process:

- Documents Required: Passport, birth certificate, police clearance, medical examination, and proof of financial solvency.
- Processing Time: Typically takes several months, so start early.

Pro Tip: Hiring a local lawyer specializing in immigration can streamline the process and help navigate bureaucratic hurdles.

For detailed information, visit the [Dominican Republic's Ministry of Foreign Affairs](https://www.mirex.gob.do/).

Political Stability

The Dominican Republic boasts a stable political environment, which is crucial for ensuring a secure and peaceful life abroad.

Government Structure:

- Democratic Republic: The DR operates as a representative democracy with executive, legislative, and judicial branches.
   - Current Leadership: The current president, Luis Abinader, took office in August 2020, focusing on economic reforms, anti-corruption measures, and improving public services.

Political Climate:

- Stability: While political protests and demonstrations occur occasionally, they are generally peaceful and pose no significant risk to expats.
   - International Relations: The DR maintains friendly relations with the U.S., EU, and other key global players, fostering a favorable environment for international residents and investors.

For more information, explore [Dominican Today](https://www.dominicantoday.com/) for the latest news and updates.

Cultural Richness

The DR's cultural tapestry is a vibrant blend of African, Taino, and European influences, offering a unique and enriching experience.

Festivals and Traditions:

- Carnival: Held every February, Carnival is a spectacular celebration featuring parades, music, dance, and colorful costumes.
    - Merengue and Bachata: These are the heartbeats of Dominican music and dance. You'll hear them everywhere, from street corners to upscale clubs.

Cuisine:

- Local Dishes: Savor traditional dishes like "La Bandera" (rice, beans, and meat), "Sancocho" (hearty stew), and "Mangu" (mashed plantains).
    - Seafood: The DR offers an abundance of fresh seafood, including grilled fish, shrimp, and lobster.

Pro Tip: Engaging with local culture through festivals, music, and cuisine is a fantastic way to integrate and make meaningful connections.

Success Stories from Expats

John and Emily, Retirees from Florida:

- Journey: John and Emily moved to the DR five years ago after retiring. They were drawn by the warm climate, affordable cost of living, and friendly locals.
    - Experience: They settled in Sosúa, a coastal town known for its expat community. "We've never felt more at home," says Emily. "The community is welcoming, and we've made friends from all over the world."

Carlos, Entrepreneur from Canada:

- Journey: Carlos relocated to Santo Domingo to start a tech company. The DR's strategic location and improving internet infrastructure were key factors.
    - Experience: "The business environment here is dynamic," Carlos shares. "There are challenges, but the opportunities outweigh them. Plus, living in such a beautiful place is a huge bonus."

For more personal stories and tips, join the [Expats in Dominican Republic](https://www.facebook.com/groups/ExpatsinDominicanRepublic/) Facebook group.

Country-Specific Tips and Advice

Housing:

- Options: From beachfront villas to mountain retreats and city apartments, the DR offers diverse housing options.
    - Cost: Housing is affordable compared to North America and Europe. A two-bedroom apartment in Santo Domingo can range from $500 to $1,500 per month, depending on location and amenities.

Healthcare:

- System: The DR has both public and private healthcare systems. Private healthcare is recommended for expats due to higher standards and shorter wait times.
    - Insurance: Health insurance is essential. Many expats opt

for international health insurance plans that provide comprehensive coverage.

Language:

- Spanish: The official language is Spanish. While many locals speak English, especially in tourist areas, learning basic Spanish will enhance your experience and integration.

Safety:

- Common Sense: As with any country, safety varies by location. Urban areas may have higher crime rates, so it's wise to stay in well-populated, secure neighborhoods.
    - Community: Engage with local expat communities for tips and advice on safe living areas and practices.

Transportation:

- Public Transport: The DR has an extensive public transportation network, including buses, taxis, and a metro system in Santo Domingo.
    - Driving: Renting or buying a car is a convenient option for exploring the island. Be prepared for local driving habits, which can be more chaotic than in the U.S. or Canada.

For more tips and resources, check out [ExpatExchange](https://www.expatexchange.com/dominican-republic/living-in-dominican-republic.html).

Resources for Further Research and Connection

Here are some valuable resources to help you plan your move and connect with the expat community in the Dominican Republic:

- Expat Forums: Websites like [ExpatExchange](https://www.expatexchange.com/dominican-republic) and [InterNations](https://www.internations.org/dominican-republic-expats) offer forums where you can ask questions and get advice from current expats.
    - Facebook Groups: Join groups such as [Expats in Dominican Republic](https://www.facebook.com/groups/ExpatsinDominicanRepublic/) to connect with others and stay updated on local events and news.
    - Government Websites: Visit the [Dominican Republic's Ministry of Foreign Affairs](https://www.mirex.gob.do/) for the latest information on visa and residency requirements.
    - Local Services: Utilize services like local real estate agents, lawyers, and relocation consultants to assist with the logistics of your move.

The Dominican Republic is more than just a tropical paradise; it's a land of opportunity, culture, and community. By understanding the legal landscape, appreciating the political stability, immersing yourself in the rich culture, and connecting with fellow expats, you can build a fulfilling and exciting new life here. So, pack your bags, embrace the adventure, and get ready to live your dream in the DR.

Ghana: Discover the Vibrant Heartbeat of Africa

People, let's take a moment to celebrate the vibrant, ever-pulsating essence of Ghana—a land where ancient traditions meet modern dynamism, creating a rich tapestry of life. Ghana isn't just a place on the map; it's a destination of dreams, an embrace of warmth, and a cradle of opportunities. Whether you're looking to immerse yourself in its cultural heritage, seek economic ventures, or find a serene spot to call home, Ghana has it all. So, let's dive deep into what makes this West African jewel an exceptional choice for those looking to escape the matrix and build a new life abroad.

Legal Considerations

Visa and Residency Requirements

Navigating the visa and residency landscape is your first step toward making Ghana your new home. Here's what you need to know:

Tourist Visa:

- Duration: Most visitors need a visa to enter Ghana. Tourist visas are typically issued for up to 90 days.
   - Extension: You can extend your stay by applying for an extension at the [Ghana Immigration Service](https://www.ghanaimmigration.org/).

Residency Visa:

- Types: Ghana offers several types of residency permits, including temporary and permanent residency.
   - Temporary Residency: Ideal for those planning to stay more than 90 days but less than a year. Applications must be made at the Ghana Immigration Service.
   - Permanent Residency: Available for those who have lived in Ghana for several years, have Ghanaian ancestry, or have invested significantly in the country.

Application Process:

- Documents Required: Passport, birth certificate, police clearance, medical examination, and proof of financial solvency.
   - Processing Time: The process can take several months, so early application is advisable.

Pro Tip: Engaging a local immigration lawyer can greatly simplify the application process and help you navigate any bureaucratic challenges.

Political Stability

Ghana's reputation for political stability is one of its many attractions, providing a secure and peaceful environment for expats.

Government Structure:

- Democratic Republic: Ghana operates as a democratic republic with executive, legislative, and judicial branches.
    - Current Leadership: President Nana Akufo-Addo, in office since January 2017, focuses on economic growth, anti-corruption measures, and improving public services.

Political Climate:

- Stability: Ghana has a strong tradition of peaceful elections and democratic transitions, making it one of Africa's most stable democracies.
    - International Relations: Ghana maintains friendly relations with many countries, including the U.S., UK, and EU nations, fostering a welcoming environment for international residents and investors.

For the latest political updates, check out [GhanaWeb](https://www.ghanaweb.com/).

Cultural Richness

Ghana's culture is a vivid blend of traditional African heritage and modern influences, creating a unique and enriching experience.

Festivals and Traditions:

- Homowo Festival: Celebrated by the Ga people, this festival features traditional music, dance, and feasting.
    - Pan-African Festival (PANAFEST): A biennial festival that celebrates African culture and promotes unity among people of African descent.

Cuisine:

- Local Dishes: Delight in traditional dishes like "Jollof Rice" (rice cooked with tomatoes, onions, and spices), "Banku" (fermented corn and cassava dough), and "Kelewele" (spicy fried plantains).
    - Street Food: Experience the vibrant street food scene with offerings like grilled tilapia, waakye (rice and beans), and fried yam.

Pro Tip: Engage with local culture through festivals, food, and community events to enrich your experience and make meaningful connections.

For more cultural insights, visit [Visit Ghana](https://visitghana.com/).

Success Stories from Expats

Samantha and Robert, Entrepreneurs from the UK:

- Journey: Samantha and Robert moved to Ghana five years ago to start a business. They were attracted by the economic opportunities and the vibrant culture.
    - Experience: They settled in Accra, the capital city. "Ghana

has been incredibly welcoming," says Samantha. "We've built a successful business and a wonderful community here."

David, Retiree from Canada:

- Journey: David relocated to Cape Coast to enjoy his retirement in a warm and friendly environment.
    - Experience: "The cost of living is affordable, and the people are so kind," David shares. "I feel like I've found my paradise."

For more personal stories, check out [InterNations Ghana](https://www.internations.org/ghana-expats).

Country-Specific Tips and Advice

Living in Ghana comes with its unique set of perks and experiences. Here's how to make the most of your time in this beautiful country.

Housing:

- Options: From modern apartments in Accra to beachside villas in Cape Coast and traditional homes in smaller towns, Ghana offers a range of housing options.
    - Cost: Housing is affordable compared to many Western countries. A two-bedroom apartment in Accra can range from $300 to $1,500 per month, depending on the location and amenities.

Healthcare:

- System: Ghana has both public and private healthcare systems. Private healthcare is recommended for expats due to higher standards and shorter wait times.

  - Insurance: Health insurance is essential. Many expats opt for international health insurance plans that provide comprehensive coverage.

Language:

- English: The official language is English, making communication relatively easy for English-speaking expats.

  - Local Languages: Learning basic phrases in local languages like Twi or Ga can enhance your experience and help build rapport with locals.

Safety:

- Common Sense: As with any country, safety varies by location. Urban areas may have higher crime rates, so it's wise to stay in well-populated, secure neighborhoods.

  - Community: Engage with local expat communities for tips and advice on safe living areas and practices.

Transportation:

- Public Transport: Ghana has an extensive public transportation network, including buses, tro-tros (minibuses), and taxis.

  - Driving: Renting or buying a car is a convenient option for exploring the country. Be prepared for local driving conditions, which can be challenging.

For practical living tips, explore [Expat Exchange](https://www.expatexchange.com/ghana).

Resources for Further Research and Connection

Here are some valuable resources to help you plan your move and connect with the expat community in Ghana:

- Expat Forums: Websites like [ExpatExchange](https://www.expatexchange.com/ghana) and [InterNations](https://www.internations.org/ghana-expats) offer forums where you can ask questions and get advice from current expats.
    - Facebook Groups: Join groups such as [Expats in Ghana](https://www.facebook.com/groups/expatsinghana/) to connect with others and stay updated on local events and news.
    - Government Websites: Visit the [Ghana Immigration Service](https://www.ghanaimmigration.org/) for the latest information on visa and residency requirements.
    - Local Services: Utilize services like local real estate agents, lawyers, and relocation consultants to assist with the logistics of your move.

Ghana is more than just a destination; it's a place where you can build a fulfilling and exciting new life. By understanding the legal landscape, appreciating the political stability, immersing yourself in the rich culture, and connecting with fellow expats, you can create a home in Ghana that offers warmth, opportunity, and a vibrant community. So, get ready to embark on this adventure and discover the endless possibilities that await you in Ghana.

Spain: Europe's Crown Jewel

Welcome to Spain, a country renowned for its rich history, vibrant culture, and exceptional quality of life. Spain offers a diverse array of experiences, from the sun-soaked beaches of the Costa del Sol to the bustling streets of Madrid and the artistic vibe of Barcelona. This Mediterranean gem is an excellent choice for expats seeking a blend of modern amenities and traditional charm. Let's dive deep into what makes Spain an exceptional place to start your new life.

Legal Landscape

- Visa and Residency Requirements

Understanding the visa and residency requirements is crucial for planning a long-term stay in Spain.

-Tourist Visa:-
  - -Duration:- Visitors from many countries, including the U.S., Canada, and EU nations, can enter Spain without a visa for up to 90 days within a 180-day period.
  - -Schengen Area:- As Spain is part of the Schengen Area, this 90-day limit applies to travel within all Schengen countries.

-Residency Visa:-

- -Types:- Spain offers several types of residency permits, including temporary and permanent residency, as well as special visas for investors and retirees.

- -Non-Lucrative Visa:- Ideal for retirees and those who do not plan to work in Spain. Requires proof of sufficient financial resources and private health insurance.

- -Golden Visa:- Available to those who invest at least €500,000 in Spanish real estate. This visa allows residency and the ability to work in Spain.

- -Work Visa:- Necessary for those planning to work in Spain. Requires a job offer and sponsorship from a Spanish employer.

-Application Process:-

- -Documents Required:- Passport, proof of financial resources, health insurance, and, for work visas, a job offer or contract.

- -Processing Time:- The process can take several months, so it's advisable to start early.

-Pro Tip:- Hiring a local immigration lawyer can greatly simplify the application process and help navigate any bureaucratic challenges.

Political Stability

Spain is known for its stable political environment, which is essential for ensuring a secure and peaceful expat life.

-Government Structure:-

- -Parliamentary Monarchy:- Spain operates as a parliamentary constitutional monarchy with executive, legislative, and judicial branches.

- -Current Leadership:- The current Prime Minister is Pedro Sánchez, who has been in office since June 2018. His administration focuses on economic growth, social welfare, and political stability.

-Political Climate:-

- -Stability:- Spain has a strong tradition of democracy and peaceful transitions of power. While political protests occur occasionally, they are generally peaceful and do not pose a significant risk to expats.

- -International Relations:- Spain maintains friendly relations with many countries, fostering a welcoming environment for international residents and investors.

Cultural Richness

Spain's culture is a vibrant blend of historical influences and modern trends, offering a unique and enriching experience.

-Festivals and Traditions:-

- -La Tomatina:- Held in Buñol, this famous festival involves a massive tomato fight and attracts participants from around the world.

- -Feria de Abril:- Seville's April Fair is a week-long celebration featuring flamenco dancing, traditional costumes, and parades.

- -San Fermín:- Known for the Running of the Bulls in Pamplona, this festival is both exhilarating and culturally significant.

-Cuisine:-

- -Local Dishes:- Savor traditional dishes like "Paella" (rice dish with seafood or meat), "Tapas" (small appetizers), and "Gazpacho" (cold tomato soup).

- -Wine:- Spain is renowned for its wine, particularly from regions like Rioja, Ribera del Duero, and Priorat.

-Pro Tip:- Engage with local culture through festivals, food, and community events to enrich your experience and make meaningful connections.

Success Stories from Expats

Here are some inspiring stories from expats who have successfully made Spain their home.

-Linda and Mark, Retirees from the U.S.:-

- -Journey:- Linda and Mark moved to the Costa del Sol five years ago to enjoy their retirement. They were attracted by the warm climate, affordable cost of living, and the friendly locals.

- -Experience:- They settled in Málaga, a city known for its beaches and vibrant cultural scene. "We've found our paradise here," says Mark. "The lifestyle is relaxed, and we've made wonderful friends."

-Emma, Digital Nomad from the UK:-

- -Journey:- Emma relocated to Barcelona to take advantage of the city's dynamic tech scene and vibrant culture.

- -Experience:- "Barcelona has the perfect mix of work and play," Emma shares. "The city is lively, and there's always something to do. Plus, the beach is just a stone's throw away."

Country-Specific Tips and Advice

Living in Spain comes with its own set of advantages and unique experiences. Here's how to make the most of your time there.

-Housing:-
 - -Options:- From modern apartments in bustling cities to charming countryside villas and coastal homes, Spain offers a wide range of housing options.
 - -Cost:- Housing costs vary significantly by location. For example, a two-bedroom apartment in Madrid or Barcelona can range from €800 to €2,500 per month, while similar accommodations in smaller cities or rural areas may cost significantly less.

-Healthcare:-
 - -System:- Spain has both public and private healthcare systems. Public healthcare is highly regarded, and private healthcare offers shorter wait times and more personalized care.
 - -Insurance:- Health insurance is essential. Many expats opt for private health insurance plans that provide comprehensive coverage.

-Language:-
 - -Spanish:- The official language is Spanish, but many people in tourist areas and major cities speak English. Learning basic Spanish will enhance your experience and integration.
 - -Regional Languages:- In some regions, you'll encounter additional languages such as Catalan in Catalonia, Basque in the Basque Country, and Galician in Galicia.

-Safety:-

- -Common Sense:- As with any country, safety varies by location. Urban areas may have higher petty crime rates, so it's wise to stay in well-populated, secure neighborhoods.

- -Community:- Engage with local expat communities for tips and advice on safe living areas and practices.

-Transportation:-

- -Public Transport:- Spain has an extensive and efficient public transportation network, including buses, trains, and metro systems in major cities.

- -Driving:- Renting or buying a car is a convenient option for exploring the country. Be prepared for local driving habits, which can be different from what you're used to.

Cities for Expats

Spain offers several cities that are particularly attractive to expats. Here are a few top choices:

-Madrid:-

- -Overview:- Spain's capital is a bustling metropolis with a rich history, vibrant culture, and a thriving business environment.

- -Attractions:- Prado Museum, Royal Palace, Retiro Park.

- -Expat Community:- Madrid has a large and active expat community, offering numerous social and professional networking opportunities.

-Barcelona:-

- -Overview:- Known for its unique architecture, beautiful

beaches, and lively arts scene, Barcelona is a favorite among expats.

- -Attractions:- Sagrada Familia, Park Güell, Gothic Quarter.

- -Expat Community:- Barcelona has a diverse and dynamic expat community, particularly appealing to digital nomads and entrepreneurs.

-Valencia:-

- -Overview:- Valencia combines historic charm with modern amenities. It's known for its festivals, cuisine, and relaxed lifestyle.

- -Attractions:- City of Arts and Sciences, Turia Gardens, Central Market.

- -Expat Community:- Valencia has a growing expat community, drawn by its lower cost of living and high quality of life.

-Seville:-

- -Overview:- Seville is the heart of Andalusia, known for its flamenco dancing, historic architecture, and warm climate.

- -Attractions:- Alcázar of Seville, Seville Cathedral, Plaza de España.

- -Expat Community:- Seville has a friendly expat community, and its slower pace of life appeals to those seeking a more traditional Spanish experience.

-Málaga:-

- -Overview:- Located on the Costa del Sol, Málaga offers stunning beaches, a vibrant cultural scene, and excellent weather.

- -Attractions:- Picasso Museum, Alcazaba, Málaga Cathedral.

- -Expat Community:- Málaga is popular with retirees and those seeking a coastal lifestyle, and it boasts a significant expat population.

Resources for Further Research and Connection

Here are some valuable resources to help you plan your move and connect with the expat community in Spain:

- -Expat Forums:- Websites like ExpatExchange and Internations offer forums where you can ask questions and get advice from current expats.
- -Facebook Groups:- Join groups such as "Expats in Spain" to connect with others and stay updated on local events and news.
- -Government Websites:- Visit Spain's Ministry of Foreign Affairs website for the latest information on visa and residency requirements.
- -Local Services: Utilize services like local real estate agents, lawyers, and relocation consultants to assist with the logistics of your move.

Spain is more than just a destination; it's a place where you can build a fulfilling and exciting new life. By understanding the legal landscape, appreciating the political stability, immersing yourself in the rich culture, and connecting with fellow expats, you can create a home in Spain that offers warmth, opportunity, and a vibrant community. So, get ready to embark on this adventure and discover the endless possibilities that await you in Spain.

Mexico: A Great Place to Escape

Mexico is more than just a destination; it's a place where you can craft a fulfilling and exciting new life. With its rich cultural heritage, diverse landscapes, and warm-hearted people, Mexico offers a welcoming environment for expats looking to start a new chapter. Let's explore what makes Mexico the ideal place to live, from understanding the legal landscape to appreciating its political stability, immersing yourself in its rich culture, and connecting with a thriving expat community.

Legal Landscape

Visa and Residency Requirements

Understanding the visa and residency requirements is essential for planning your long-term stay in Mexico.

Tourist Visa:
   - Duration: Most visitors can enter Mexico without a visa for up to 180 days.
   - Extension: Extensions are generally not available for tourist visas, so planning your transition to a residency visa is key if you wish to stay longer.

Residency Visa:

- Temporary Residency: Suitable for those planning to stay longer than six months but less than four years. You can apply at a Mexican consulate in your home country or switch from a tourist visa while in Mexico.

- Permanent Residency: Available for those who have held a temporary residency for four years or meet specific criteria, such as retirement or financial solvency.

Application Process:

- Documents Required: Passport, proof of income, bank statements, and a completed application form.

- Processing Time: The process can take several weeks to a few months, so starting early is advisable.

Pro Tip: Hiring a local immigration lawyer can greatly simplify the application process and help you navigate any bureaucratic challenges. For detailed information, visit the [Instituto Nacional de Migración](https://www.inm.gob.mx/).

Political Stability

Mexico's political environment is generally stable, providing a secure setting for expats.

Government Structure:

- Federal Republic: Mexico operates as a federal republic with executive, legislative, and judicial branches.

- Current Leadership: President Andrés Manuel López Obrador has been in office since December 2018, focusing on economic reform and social development.

Political Climate:

- Stability: While there are occasional protests and political movements, they are generally peaceful and do not pose a significant risk to expats.

- International Relations: Mexico maintains strong ties with the U.S., Canada, and many other countries, fostering a favorable environment for international residents and investors.

For the latest political updates, check out [Mexico News Daily](https://mexiconewsdaily.com/).

Cultural Richness

Mexico's culture is a vibrant blend of indigenous heritage and Spanish influence, offering an enriching experience.

Festivals and Traditions:

- Día de los Muertos (Day of the Dead): Celebrated in early November, this colorful and heartfelt festival honors deceased loved ones.

- Cinco de Mayo: Commemorates the Mexican army's victory over the French at the Battle of Puebla.

Cuisine:

- Local Dishes: Indulge in traditional dishes like tacos al pastor, mole poblano, and tamales.

- Street Food: Savor the vibrant street food scene with treats like elotes (grilled corn), churros, and quesadillas.

Pro Tip: Engage with local culture through festivals, food, and community events to enrich your experience and make meaningful connections. For more cultural insights, visit [Visit

Mexico](https://www.visitmexico.com/).

Success Stories from Expats

Emma and Jack, Entrepreneurs from the U.S.:
   - Journey: Emma and Jack moved to Mexico City five years ago to start a tech company. They were drawn by the economic opportunities and vibrant lifestyle.
   - Experience: "Mexico has been incredibly welcoming," says Emma. "We've built a successful business and a wonderful community here."
   Maria, Retiree from Canada:
   - Journey: Maria relocated to San Miguel de Allende to enjoy her retirement in a warm and friendly environment.
   - Experience: "The cost of living is affordable, and the people are so kind," Maria shares. "I feel like I've found my paradise."

For more personal stories, check out [Expat Exchange](https://www.expatexchange.com/mexico).

Country-Specific Tips and Advice

Living in Mexico comes with its unique set of perks and experiences. Here's how to make the most of your time in this beautiful country.

Housing:
   - Options: From modern apartments in Mexico City to beachfront villas in Cancún and charming homes in colonial towns, Mexico offers a range of housing options.
   - Cost: Housing is affordable compared to many Western

countries. A two-bedroom apartment in Mexico City can range from $500 to $2,000 per month, depending on the location and amenities.

Healthcare:

- System: Mexico has both public and private healthcare systems. Private healthcare is recommended for expats due to higher standards and shorter wait times.

- Insurance: Health insurance is essential. Many expats opt for international health insurance plans that provide comprehensive coverage.

Language:

- Spanish: The official language is Spanish. While many locals speak English, especially in tourist areas, learning basic Spanish will enhance your experience and integration.

Safety:

- Common Sense: As with any country, safety varies by location. Urban areas may have higher crime rates, so it's wise to stay in well-populated, secure neighborhoods.

- Community: Engage with local expat communities for tips and advice on safe living areas and practices.

Transportation:

- Public Transport: Mexico has an extensive public transportation network, including buses, metro systems in larger cities, and taxis.

- Driving: Renting or buying a car is a convenient option for exploring the country. Be prepared for local driving conditions, which can be challenging.

For practical living tips, explore [Expat Exchange](https://w

ww.expatexchange.com/mexico).

Resources for Further Research and Connection

Here are some valuable resources to help you plan your move and connect with the expat community in Mexico:

- Expat Forums: Websites like [ExpatExchange](https://www.expatexchange.com/mexico) and [InterNations](https://www.internations.org/mexico-expats) offer forums where you can ask questions and get advice from current expats.

- Facebook Groups: Join groups such as [Expats in Mexico](https://www.facebook.com/groups/expatsinmexico/) to connect with others and stay updated on local events and news.e in Mexico that offers warmth, opportunity, and a vibrant community. So, get ready to embark on this

- Government Websites: Visit the [Instituto Nacional de Migración](https://www.inm.gob.mx/) for the latest information on visa and residency requirements.

- Local Services: Utilize services like local real estate agents, lawyers, and relocation consultants to assist with the logistics of your move.

Mexico is more than just a destination; it's a place where you can build a fulfilling and exciting new life. By understanding the legal landscape, appreciating the political stability, immersing yourself in the rich culture, and connecting with fellow expats, you can create a hom adventure and discover the endless possibilities that await you in Mexico.

Thailand: Southeast Asia's Finest

Ladies and gentlemen, let's take a moment to celebrate the vibrant, ever-pulsating essence of Thailand—a land where ancient traditions meet modern dynamism, creating a rich tapestry of life. Thailand isn't just a place on the map; it's a destination of dreams, an embrace of warmth, and a cradle of opportunities. Whether you're looking to immerse yourself in its cultural heritage, seek economic ventures, or find a serene spot to call home, Thailand has it all. So, let's dive deep into what makes this Southeast Asian jewel an exceptional choice for those looking to escape the matrix and build a new life abroad.

Legal Landscape

Visa and Residency Requirements

Navigating the visa and residency landscape is your first step toward making Thailand your new home. Here's what you need to know:

Tourist Visa:

- Duration: Most visitors need a visa to enter Thailand. Tourist visas are typically issued for up to 60 days.

- Extension: You can extend your stay by applying for an extension at the [Thai Immigration Bureau](https://www.imm igration.go.th/).

Residency Visa:

- Types: Thailand offers several types of residency permits, including temporary and permanent residency.
    - Temporary Residency: Ideal for those planning to stay more than 60 days but less than a year. Applications must be made at the Thai Immigration Bureau.
    - Permanent Residency: Available for those who have lived in Thailand for several years, have Thai ancestry, or have invested significantly in the country.

Application Process:

- Documents Required: Passport, birth certificate, police clear-ance, medical examination, and proof of financial solvency.
    - Processing Time: The process can take several months, so early application is advisable.

Pro Tip: Engaging a local immigration lawyer can greatly simplify the application process and help you navigate any bureaucratic challenges.

Political Stability

Thailand's reputation for political stability is one of its many attractions, providing a secure and peaceful environment for expats.

Government Structure:

- Constitutional Monarchy: Thailand operates as a constitutional monarchy with executive, legislative, and judicial branches.
   - Current Leadership: The current Prime Minister is Prayut Chan-o-cha. His administration focuses on economic growth, anti-corruption measures, and improving public services.

Political Climate:

- Stability: Thailand has a strong tradition of peaceful elections and democratic transitions, making it one of Southeast Asia's most stable democracies.
   - International Relations: Thailand maintains friendly relations with many countries, including the U.S., UK, and EU nations, fostering a welcoming environment for international residents and investors.

For the latest political updates, check out [Bangkok Post](https://www.bangkokpost.com/).

Cultural Richness

Thailand's culture is a vivid blend of traditional Asian heritage and modern influences, creating a unique and enriching experience.

Festivals and Traditions:

- Songkran Festival: Celebrated in April, this festival marks the Thai New Year with water fights, traditional music, and dance.
   - Loy Krathong: Held in November, this festival involves floating lanterns and offerings on rivers and lakes to honor the water spirits.

Cuisine:

- Local Dishes: Delight in traditional dishes like "Pad Thai" (stir-fried noodles), "Tom Yum Goong" (spicy shrimp soup), and "Som Tum" (papaya salad).
   - Street Food: Experience the vibrant street food scene with offerings like mango sticky rice, satay, and coconut ice cream.

Pro Tip: Engage with local culture through festivals, food, and community events to enrich your experience and make meaningful connections.

For more cultural insights, visit [Tourism Authority of Thailand](https://www.tourismthailand.org/).

Success Stories from Expats

Susan and Robert, Entrepreneurs from the UK:

- Journey: Susan and Robert moved to Thailand five years ago to start a business. They were attracted by the economic opportunities and the vibrant culture.
   - Experience: They settled in Bangkok, the capital city. "Thailand has been incredibly welcoming," says Susan. "We've built a successful business and a wonderful community here."

David, Retiree from Canada:

- Journey: David relocated to Chiang Mai to enjoy his retirement in a warm and friendly environment.
    - Experience: "The cost of living is affordable, and the people are so kind," David shares. "I feel like I've found my paradise."

For more personal stories, check out [InterNations Thailand](https://www.internations.org/thailand-expats).

Country-Specific Tips and Advice

Living in Thailand comes with its unique set of perks and experiences. Here's how to make the most of your time in this beautiful country.

Housing:

- Options: From modern apartments in Bangkok to beachside villas in Phuket and traditional homes in smaller towns, Thailand offers a range of housing options.
    - Cost: Housing is affordable compared to many Western countries. A two-bedroom apartment in Bangkok can range from $300 to $1,500 per month, depending on the location and amenities.

Healthcare:

- System: Thailand has both public and private healthcare systems. Private healthcare is recommended for expats due to higher standards and shorter wait times.

- Insurance: Health insurance is essential. Many expats opt for international health insurance plans that provide comprehensive coverage.

Language:

- Thai: The official language is Thai, making communication easier if you learn some basic phrases.
    - English: While English is widely spoken in tourist areas, learning basic Thai will enhance your experience and help build rapport with locals.

Safety:

- Common Sense: As with any country, safety varies by location. Urban areas may have higher crime rates, so it's wise to stay in well-populated, secure neighborhoods.
    - Community: Engage with local expat communities for tips and advice on safe living areas and practices.

Transportation:

- Public Transport: Thailand has an extensive public transportation network, including buses, skytrains, and tuk-tuks.
    - Driving: Renting or buying a car is a convenient option for exploring the country. Be prepared for local driving conditions, which can be challenging.

For practical living tips, explore [Expat Exchange](https://www.expatexchange.com/thailand).

Resources for Further Research and Connection

Here are some valuable resources to help you plan your move and connect with the expat community in Thailand:

- Expat Forums: Websites like [ExpatExchange](https://www.expatexchange.com/thailand) and [InterNations](https://www.internations.org/thailand-expats) offer forums where you can ask questions and get advice from current expats.
    - Facebook Groups: Join groups such as [Expats in Thailand](https://www.facebook.com/groups/expatsinthailand/) to connect with others and stay updated on local events and news.
    - Government Websites: Visit the [Thai Immigration Bureau](https://www.immigration.go.th/) for the latest information on visa and residency requirements.
    - Local Services: Utilize services like local real estate agents, lawyers, and relocation consultants to assist with the logistics of your move.

Thailand is more than just a destination; it's a place where you can build a fulfilling and exciting new life. By understanding the legal landscape, appreciating the political stability, immersing yourself in the rich culture, and connecting with fellow expats, you can create a home in Thailand that offers warmth, opportunity, and a vibrant community. So, get ready to embark on this adventure and discover the endless possibilities that await you in Thailand.

Embrace Your Journey to Freedom

Folks, as we come to the end of this guide, let's take a moment to reflect on the journey we've embarked upon together. We've navigated through the essential steps of creating a stable base, securing your assets, and exploring expat-friendly destinations around the world. We've delved into the legal, political, and cultural landscapes of ten remarkable countries, each offering unique opportunities for a fulfilling life abroad. Now, it's time to bring it all together and look forward to the adventures that lie ahead.

First and foremost, we started by understanding the importance of establishing a solid foundation in your home country. We assessed our current situation, planned for financial stability, built a support network, and maintained essential relationships. These steps are crucial because they ensure you have a strong anchor as you venture into new territories.

Next, we moved on to securing your assets. We discussed organizing your finances, planning investments, understanding legal considerations, and ensuring easy access to funds abroad. These steps are vital for protecting your wealth and ensuring a smooth transition as you relocate.

We then explored how to research and choose the best destinations for expat life. By identifying your needs and preferences, leveraging resources for research, and considering key factors like cost of living and healthcare, you're equipped to make informed decisions. Making initial contact with expat communities further eases the transition and helps you integrate into your new environment.

We also delved into the legal landscape of your new home, discussing visa and residency requirements, work permits, tax implications, and navigating foreign legal systems. Understanding these aspects is crucial to avoid any legal pitfalls and ensure a hassle-free experience.

Cultural adaptation is another cornerstone of successful expat life. Embracing cultural differences, learning the local language, building relationships with locals, and integrating into the community enrich your experience and help you truly become a part of your new home.

Now, let me tell you something, folks. As you stand on the brink of this incredible journey, you might feel a mix of excitement and apprehension. That's perfectly natural. Stepping out of your comfort zone and embracing a new way of life is no small feat. But remember, the rewards are immeasurable.

Picture yourself walking along the cobblestone streets of Las Catalinas in Guanacaste, Costa Rica, with the sun kissing your face and the ocean breeze gently whispering in your ear. Imagine sipping coffee at a quaint café in Istanbul, where the aroma of freshly brewed coffee mingles with the rich history that surrounds you. Envision the vibrant festivals and warm smiles of the Dominican Republic, where every day feels like a celebration of life.

The world is full of wonders waiting to be explored, and by escaping the matrix, you're giving yourself the gift of freedom. You're choosing to live life on your own terms, to discover new cultures, and to create a legacy that transcends borders.

As you embark on this journey, know that you're not alone. There are countless resources and communities ready to support you every step of the way. Here are some valuable references to keep in your back pocket:

- -Expat Forums:- Websites like Expat.com and Internations offer forums where you can ask questions, share experiences, and connect with fellow expats.
    - -Facebook Groups:- Join groups such as "Expats in Dominican Republic" to stay updated on local events and find a supportive community.
    - -Government Websites:- Visit the official immigration websites of your chosen country for the latest information on visas and residency requirements.
    - -Local Services:- Utilize local real estate agents, immigration consultants, and relocation services to assist with your move.

So, my friends, as you set sail on this new adventure, carry with you the wisdom, courage, and humor we've shared in these pages. Remember that the world is your oyster, and with determination and an open heart, you can create a life filled with joy, purpose, and endless possibilities.

In the words of Dave Chappelle, "Sometimes you gotta take a leap and build your wings on the way down." And as Bernie Mac would say, "Don't be scared. The world is out there waiting for you to conquer it."

We're global now, folks. Get out there and make your marks. And remember the best is yet to come.

www.ingramcontent.com/pod-product-compliance
Lightning Source LLC
Chambersburg PA
CBHW071222260726
48653CB00042B/1533